The
Fast Forward
MBA in Selling

THE FAST FORWARD MBA SERIES

The Fast Forward MBA Series provides time-pressed business professionals and students with concise, one-stop information to help them solve business problems and make smart, informed business decisions. All of the volumes, written by industry leaders, contain "tough ideas made easy." The published books in this series are:

The Fast Forward MBA in Business
(0-471-14660-9)
by Virginia O'Brien

The Fast Forward MBA in Finance
(0-471-10930-4)
by John Tracy

The Fast Forward MBA Pocket Reference
(0-471-14595-5)
by Paul A. Argenti

The Fast Forward MBA in Marketing
(0-471-16616-2)
by Dallas Murphy

The Fast Forward MBA in Hiring
(0-471-24212-8)
by Max Messmer

The Fast Forward MBA in Project Management
(0-471-32546-5)
by Eric Verzuh

The Fast Forward MBA in Business
Communication
(0-471-32731-x)
by Lauren Vicker & Ron Hein

The Fast Forward MBA in Business Planning
for Growth
(0-471-34548-2)
by Philip Walcoff

The Fast Forward MBA in Selling

Become a Self-Motivated Profit-Center—and Prosper

JOY J. D. BALDRIDGE

John Wiley & Sons, Inc.

z

New York • Chichester • Weinheim • Brisbane • Singapore • Toronto

This publication is designed to provide accurate and authoritative
information in regard to the subject matter covered. It is sold
with the understanding that the publisher is not engaged in
rendering legal, accounting, or other professional services. If
legal advice or other expert assistance is required, the services of
a competent professional person should be sought.

ISBN 0-471-34854-6

Printed in the United States of America.

10 9 8 7 6 5 4 3 2 1

*This book is dedicated with love
to Ken, Lila, Bill, Wilson, Jonas, Jesse, Bob,
Liz, Luke, Cliff, Mary, Dottie, and Grace.*

JOY J. D. BALDRIDGE

Joy J. D. Baldridge is president of Baldridge Seminars International, a Connecticut-based training organization that focuses on sales, customer service, and management skill development both domestically and globally.

Ms. Baldridge obtained her sales and management training experience first in advertising sales and then in sales recruiting, where she interviewed more than 6,000 sales candidates and placed over 800 of them in sales positions. As a sales professional, she has made over a quarter of a million cold calls, which led her to become the number one revenue producer at each corporation where she sold.

Her corporate training experience began in 1981 as a trainer at Baldridge Reading and Study Skills, Inc., an educational organization founded by her parents in 1956. She founded Baldridge Seminars International in 1989. She was producer of *At Work with Joy Baldridge,* a cable TV talk show in which she interviewed CEOs and presidents of Fortune 500 companies regarding their formulas for achieving peak performance.

Ms. Baldridge has conducted more than 5,000 training sessions for over 200 corporations, associations, colleges, and universities, including 3M, Time Warner, Xerox, The American Management Association, the Magazine Publishers of America, and Colgate, Fairfield, Skidmore, Tulane, and Yale. One of her more interesting assignments was training the President's staff on time management and information processing strategies at The White House.

ACKNOWLEDGMENTS

In the summer of 1998 I was giving a sales seminar in New York City. During the midmorning break a young woman named Rhonda Moller came up to me and said, "This information is really good—where's your book?" When I said that I didn't have one, she gave me the name of a senior editor at her company, John Wiley & Sons, Inc. And thus started my journey into book writing.

I wish to express my sincere and lasting thanks to Rhonda Moller, as well as to the following people without whose help this book would not have been possible: To my parents, Ken and Lila Baldridge, who exchanged endless faxes and Federal Express packages with me as they hopscotched across the country teaching the Baldridge Reading Program. They always had a special and unique way of providing emotional support as well as being brilliant with words, usage, and sentence construction. To my husband and children for their patience and encouragement in giving me the freedom and time to pursue this dream.

I would also like to thank Renana Meyers for using the best of her editing wisdom and talents. Literary agent Bob Tabian's insights were invaluable. I was fortunate to have tremendously dedicated administrative support from Eileen Arndt and Barbara Zamolsky.

And thanks to Paul Masterson, Kilian Connolly, and Chris Hynes of Update Legal, who with seconds to spare helped me locate a Federal Express office in Boston to send the final, final edit to the publisher.

Writer's inspiration came from within the family tree from cousin Wendy Schuman, grandmother Dottie Denton Baldridge, and Ken and Lila Baldridge, all published authors. Business partnerships and alliances with Mark Riesenberg and Nina Merer proved invaluable. The enthusiasm of friends and neighbors was a strong motivating factor. Thanks to the Lamontes, Julie Jansen, Ben Bauer, Sue Cronin, Joann Flynn, Liz Jones, Lola Dennis, and especially Mary Schweikert. And finally, thanks and love to my Great Aunt Grace, who has always been an inspiration and always will be.

CONTENTS

CHAPTER SIX—CONDUCTING PERSUASIVE, RESULTS-DRIVEN SALES CALLS 119

**CHAPTER SEVEN—THE BEST
TECHNOLOGY FOR SUCCESSFUL
SELLING   147**

LIST OF TABLES

The world stands aside to let anyone pass who knows where he/she is going.
David Jordan

The sales profession is rapidly changing. Today the opportunity for high financial gain is better than ever. But to obtain the results you are seeking, a new set of rules applies.

The trend in business is toward an autonomous workforce, and there is no place where that is more prevalent than in sales. In the past, the sales manager was the pivotal point person in charge of hiring, motivating, guiding, reassuring, and training his or her sales force on how to be the best, how to take the lead, how to be cutting edge, how to blow out the numbers.

Today, however, we face a paradox. Fast forward to the new millennium, where the once-indispensable sales management positions are being eliminated, and sales professionals are being left to fend for themselves. With less management support, it is now necessary for sales professionals to become more strictly self-disciplined and self-driven because only the highly disciplined and self-driven will survive. This is where the concept of the self-managed sales professional begins.

Today, every sales professional must focus on becoming a self-managed, activity-driven profit center. No longer do you have the luxury of relying on your managers to be available to provide guidance, support, encouragement, and leadership. Successful, revenue-driven sales professionals will have to develop the fine skill of self-management, that is, of being your own boss and support provider.

What, exactly, is a self-managed sales professional? He or she is a person responsible for generating revenue and profit—whether selling goods or services for an organization or building his/her own business. The bottom-line characteristics of a self-managed sales professional is that he or she has an independent and primary responsibility to generate revenue.

Once you adopt and implement this book's philosophy and techniques, you'll see a positive impact on your revenue growth. *The Fast Forward MBA in Selling* contains what Joy J. D. Baldridge calls Golden Nuggets™ of information, meaning practical and useful selling formulas that are real-world tested and immediately applicable. These simple approaches will empower sales professionals who today do not have the time to pore over volumes of information detailing intricate and complex paradigms, but instead need to be out in the field building relationships and closing sales by applying user-friendly sales strategies.

This book is a coach, companion, and resource guide designed specifically for the sales professional and sales manager who wants to increase sales revenue.

The purpose of *The Fast Forward MBA in Selling* is to provide you with the proven formula necessary to become a self-managed sales professional. This book will also provide specific guidelines to assist sales managers in empowering those who make up their sales forces to become more independent decision makers, highly motivated action takers, and powerful revenue generators.

Why is the self-management approach to selling so essential right now? It is necessary in part because many sales professionals are being forced into an independent existence. They are being sent home with laptops, cell phones, and beepers to manage their territory as if it were their own business. Through new technology such as e-mail, voice mail, and the Internet, corporate America is in many cases beginning to eliminate its largest financial expenditure—real estate. Every corporation is squeezing the last penny out of each dollar for sake of increased profits. So you'll need to learn how to still prosper by successfully adapting to these changes.

Also, the role of sales managers has changed a great deal. They no longer have the time they once had to coach, mentor, nurture, support, direct, and develop their sales forces. Today the majority are also expected to be "selling" managers, strategic marketers, and financial analysts. They don't have the time to provide "all the answers." (Nor, perhaps, should they.) With the rapid changes taking place in responsibilities of sales managers, *The Fast Forward MBA in Selling* provides the latest techniques and strategies for managers to fast track the professional advancement of their sales reps while still focusing on their own new and changing roles.

Nevertheless, this is a very exciting and highly lucrative time to be in sales. The climate couldn't be better for enormous revenue growth. The key element is to think of yourself as managing your own business—managing your time, territory, growth and development, problem-solving and decision-making abilities, emotions, technology, and even your boss.

This book is a how-to guide to empower sales professionals to take their skill-sets up a notch; to make the best even better. It takes a sophisticated yet simple approach by providing an abundance of "Golden Nugget®" concepts, i.e.: concentrated ideas and powerful tools that when organized in a unique and customized form result in a system that will work for each person who reads it. There is more potential now than ever to make enormous sums of money and achieve greatness for yourself, your manager, and your parent company. The key is to begin. And the critical time is now.

Professional Selling Basics

Setting the Standards for Success

Those on the top of the mountain didn't fall there.
Marcus Washling

Self-managed selling can provide a positive and exciting future for sales representatives. It empowers them to become more autonomous in their decision making. Those who embrace self-managed selling, and succeed at it, will emerge as top-notch, quality leaders who can have a tremendous impact on the future.

Sales is an exciting and challenging profession. A successful sales regime consists of a series of techniques, strategies, and events that lead to increased revenue, profits, and commissions. With a little luck and a lot of persistence and tenacity that success can be yours.

Sales is an emotion-driven profession. It is laden with relentless cold calling, endless sales meetings, and tenacious follow-through, all in the face of unconscionable rejection. Yet, somehow, through it all, those who stick with it by adhering to essential standards that lead to success and staying on top of the challenge can end up driving corporate revenues up—along with commission dollars and customer satisfaction.

For most sales professionals, part of the reward has been in the glory of recognition. Many a time what has kept the sales professional's momentum up is encouragement and guidance from a trusted manager. Most of the strategic planning, expectation-setting, and forecasting was done by sales managers as well. But, with sales managers' roles becoming more distant and in some cases obsolete, sales professionals now have to generate their own motivation, and enhance their own skill-sets, core competencies, and standards to meet this challenge. At times they will have to take on both the role of sales representative and sales manager simultaneously.

Sales professionals traditionally have had a variety of introductions into their chosen field. Some have been fortunate enough to attend comprehensive training sessions to acquire both product and sales knowledge. Depending on the parent company and the complexity level involved in the job, sales training could consist of anything from one to two days to one to two years. But again, today the responsibility for acquiring the right knowledge and tools falls more and more onto the sales professional personally, to search for the right books to read, and select the best seminars to attend.

At the same time, the sales field has become more sophisticated to keep up with the changing times. For instance, the client/customer is becoming far more educated, so the sales professional's approach is more consultative in nature, a strategic partnering where the client and sales representatives join together to solve problems.

The benefits of making the transformation from relying on a sales manager's guidance and support to one of self-guidance and self-support are numerous. Among the greatest benefits are the confidence and satisfaction of becoming a true leader.

This chapter describes the core techniques necessary to build a solid foundation as a self-managed sales professional by setting and following standards. Once the key concepts are applied, it will become very clear how to gain the confidence and momentum necessary to achieve the results you are after. It all begins with *expectation-setting.*

Be so good they can't ignore you.
Jerry Dunn

KEY CONCEPT · SETTING EXPECTATIONS TO GET RESULTS

Expectation-setting is setting the standards for success. The key question to ask yourself before making a sale is, "What am I expecting?"

What am I expecting from myself, my prospects, my clients, and my parent company? You typically get what you expect—yet making a tangible expectation list is an activity that most sales professionals don't get around to doing.

The Five Guidelines to Expectation-Setting

Step 1. *List.* Write down what you expect of yourself as a sales professional. For example: Be energetic, knowledgeable, consultative, personable, professional, goal-oriented, profit-driven, etc.

Step 2. *Clarify.* Ask yourself what you mean by the words or phrases on your expectation list. For instance: "Knowledgeable"—meaning knowing my product; knowing key questions to ask on sales calls; knowing my customer; knowing the industry. This clarification step is critical in defining the expectations in more depth. The clearer the expectation is, the better the results will be.

Step 3. *Write.* Expectations must be in writing. Putting them in writing makes them more tangible. Just "knowing" what you expect is not good enough. Floating thoughts are far too vague. The written word is concrete and very powerful.

Step 4. *Believe.* You must believe down to the marrow of your bones that your expectations are obtainable. "What you believe to be true either is true or will become true." This is the definition of a self-fulfilling prophecy. Without a strong belief system, you'll make more errors and lose momentum, especially when setbacks strike. And there are always setbacks—expect them. Put them on your expectation list.

Step 5. *Review.* Review your expectation list daily. A quick review of what you expect of yourself reminds you of the value that you bring to the work you do. It is very easy to lose sight of your purpose, your integrity, your spirit. An expectation list keeps your values in the fore-front of your mind, and reminds you to live to your highest potential every second of the day.

Climb high, climb far, your goal the sky, your aim the star.
Unknown

Now that you are aware of the guidelines necessary to create your own list of expectations to use as standards for selling success, here we will be covering eight crucial expectations you may choose to add to your list to increase your probability for success.

EIGHT EXPECTATIONS FOR SALES SUCCESS

Expectation #1. Flexibility
    Meaning: Be adaptable
Expectation #2. Mission
    Meaning: Be focused
Expectation #3. Give and Get
    Meaning: Have mutual respect
Expectation #4. Underpromise and Overdeliver
    Meaning: Think ahead
Expectation #5. Preparation
    Meaning: Get ready
Expectation #6. Client-Focused Selling
    Meaning: Be selfless
Expectation #7. Make the Client Feel Important
    Meaning: Offer sincere praise
Expectation #8. Integrity
    Meaning: Have a code of values

 **KEY CONCEPT**

EXPECTATION #1: FLEXIBILITY

When setting expectations regarding yourself and your relationships with others, remember that one of the most important characteristics to possess is flexibility. As a matter of fact, a few years ago *Fortune* magazine stated you need to have two key characteristics to be employed in the next century. Those characteristics are *flexibility* and *adaptability*.

Setting specific expectations is the key to success, and being flexible will help you achieve them.

BOTTOM LINE **Be Flexible**

If you are rigid you will break, and your service will break down as well. If you are flexible and adaptable, you will fold your services into the fabric of your client's needs.

Reverse Your Thoughts

Oppositivity thinking is a process of reversal of thought where you replace the thought "I can't do this" with "How can I do this?"

KEY CONCEPT **EXPECTATION #2: MISSION FOR THE DAY**

Having a clear daily mission can be a driving force of your business. By asking, "What is my mission for the day?" you will develop clear and focused thoughts.

Once you set your mission for the day, you'll find that all of your efforts and activities start to migrate toward that mission.

You can also have a "mission" for each sales call, which will clearly focus your intention in a way that most sales people lack. "What is my mission for this call?" provides a laser-beam-like focus on the most critical aspects of your call (or day). This focus results in greater satisfaction and provides an abundance of tangible results.

BOTTOM LINE **Mission Equals Goals**

With a mission, you know where you're going, and you'll reach more goals.

The first and most important thing about goals is having one.
Geoffrey Albert

Mission-Minded

Ask yourself, "What is my mission for today?" at the beginning of each day. Before each sales call, ask, "What is my mission for this call?"

KEY CONCEPT **EXPECTATION #3: GIVE AND GET®**

Sales professionals tend to give too much away. (That is one major reason why sales man-

Stellar Performer: Paul Viti, Xerox Corporation
The Viti Visor

Paul Viti was a top sales professional and, later, a top sales manager at Xerox Corporation. When asked how he managed his team to such great success, he responded that he attributed it to hiring and developing self-managed people. To help train his staff to be self-managed, he developed the concept of the "Viti Visor." Paul had two bumper-sticker-like banners printed up that he would give to each sales professional to attach to the sun visors of his or her car. The driver's-side visor read, "What is your mission for this call?" The sales professional would flip the visor down before the call and mentally focus on the mission/main objective/primary goal for the sales call. After completing the call, upon returning to the car he or she would flip the visor on the passenger side of the car down to read the second bumper sticker, which said, "Did you reach your mission?"

What the Viti Visor concept demonstrates is a way for management to create a self-managed sales force by assisting the sales representatives in staying focused on their goal, and focusing on accountability. It allows for salespeople to self-coach by self-questioning. Paul could link substantial increase in revenue directly to the application of the Viti Visor.

agement exists.) If a buyer/customer/client flinches at the quoted price, the sales rep often reacts immediately with a price reduction. And price is not the only area where salespeople tend to give away too much. Time, advice, and future discounts are also needlessly given in hopes of getting the sale.

By substituting a "give-and-get" philosophy, the expectation is transformed into having a relationship that warrants mutual respect versus one in which you give and give, and get little in return.

A "give-and-get" relationship evens the playing field. It commands mutual respect. A "give, give, give" relationship makes the client feel in complete control and the salesperson feel taken advantage of.

A few examples of the "give-and-get" relationship are listed in Table 1.1

DANGER! **Avoid Obsessiveness**

The "give-and-get" philosophy is designed to have each party make *equal* contributions toward reaching a goal. Setting and applying the "give-and-get" standard allows for teamwork and effective partnering to occur. The danger occurs when you become obsessive and constantly keep track of who did what when. Focusing only on tit for tat will make you lose sight of the big picture. It is far better to keep track of the bigger goal: what you are doing and what the client is doing to work toward a mutual agreement—the sale.

**TABLE 1.1 THE GIVE-AND-GET®
PHILOSOPHY EVENS THE PLAYING
FIELD SO YOU GAIN RESPECT AND
AVOID LOSING TOO MUCH**

Scenario 1

A client asks for you to "draft and send a proposal."
Your response: "I'd be delighted to draft a proposal. I can have it ready within a week. [The give.] When can we meet to discuss it?" [The get.]

Scenario 2

A client requests that you run an event together.
Your response: "I'd be delighted to run the event with you. [The give.] Let's jot down what we can each do to make it a tremendous success." [The get.]

BOTTOM LINE Reach More Goals

The bottom line to "give-and-get" is: "I'll do this for you, if you do this for me." We both contribute our time, energy, and resources toward working successfully together to reach our goal.

KEY CONCEPT

EXPECTATION #4: UNDERPROMISE AND OVERDELIVER

Sales relationships are built on trust. When promises are not kept, trust is broken. Underpromise and overdeliver is a concept that involves thinking ahead and planning for inevitable, unforeseen obstacles.

Many sales professionals need to leave a little extra time in the equation when making a promise to a client. Most people underestimate the time it takes to fulfill commitments. There is a rule of thumb in time management: It generally takes twice as long to do something than you think it will. This is also known as the *2× rule*. So, if you think a commitment or task will take an hour, double it to two in your daily planner. In most cases promises can be prevented from being broken if you use the 2× rule. While you cannot always double your time estimate, allowing for such extra time as is reasonably available to keep a commitment will yield substantial results.

The "Wow!" Factor

One of the most positive outcomes of applying the underpromise and overdeliver concept is that it makes clients say "Wow!" When an expectation is exceeded, it makes you shine. It shows that you are different from the rest. It also allows you to keep more promises.

For instance, if you plan to *exceed* an expectation and then fall short of that goal, usually you can still keep the promise itself as well as your client's trust. But if you plan simply to keep a promise and then miss, you'll probably end up breaking the promise and jeopardizing your client's trust.

This concept reminds me of the philosophy of an eighth-grade teacher I once knew. He always said, "If you're early, you're on time. If you're on time, you're late—and if you're late, get out!"

("And you have detention!") Needless to say, I was one of the first to arrive in class throughout that year and witnessed many students receiving detentions in his class.

Based on all of the benefits listed in Table 1.2, why wouldn't you use the "underpromise and overdeliver" concept?

⬦DANGER! KNOW THE RIGHT WAYS TO WOW!

As with any tool, there are right and wrong ways to use this one. Here are some pointers for using "underpromise and overdeliver" correctly:

1. Eliminate the word "always." If you *always* plan to use this technique, it may backfire. Instead, use it strategically, when it will have the greatest impact. Adapt for crisis, crunch time. Circumstances may not allow for exceeding client expectations when a project is already in a time crunch. If a crisis is upon you, it means that just getting the job done is important and urgent and there is no time for the 2× rule to be factored in. So simply do your very best to meet the deadline.

2. Allow for a final proofing and preparation. You can deliver externally "on time," but internally have proposals and projects ready slightly ahead of schedule. This allows for extra proofing and final touches to be done. Have you ever proofed a document and discovered errors as you were faxing it or when you were waiting in the lobby of the client? Time needs to be factored in to prevent this from occurring. Finding errors ahead of time (behind the scenes) builds your credibility and your clients' confidence in

---

TABLE 1.2 THE BENEFITS OF "UNDER-PROMISE AND OVERDELIVER"

1. Less stress
2. More time
3. Room for problem-solving
4. Allows for obstacle-recovery
5. Wows your customer
6. Keeps your promise
7. Builds trust
8. Differentiates you from the rest
9. Seals the relationship

you. Finding these errors in front of the client damages your credibility.

3. Think it through. If you believe that getting information or delivering on a promise ahead of time to your client is not appropriate—don't do it. You know your client better than anyone else does. Usually exceeding an expectation is considered a positive gesture. But *not always*. You don't want the client to underappreciate your efforts because you got it done too quickly and made it look too easy (especially for the price you are charging). Go with your gut. Few people complain of having extra time to fulfill a promise, but how many times have you uttered the words with regret and frustration, "I need more time."

BOTTOM **Commitment**

LINE Underpromise/overdeliver: It's all about time, commitment, thinking ahead, preparing for unforeseen obstacles, and how you plan for keeping promises and exceeding expectations to build and strengthen relationships.

 **EXPECTATION #5: PREPARATION**

CONCEPT Preparation is the cornerstone to effective selling. It is also the key to conducting successful negotiations and presentations.

Preparation builds confidence, provides insights, and shows the client that you're knowledgeable, professional, and that you care. Yet many sales professionals still "wing it." They use the argument that they don't want to sound canned or unnatural. But their results are usually hit-or-miss.

Preparation can mean many different things. And there are a multitude of ways to prepare. Focusing on your mission is a good way to start (see Expectation #2 on page 7). Once your mission is clear, use the 10 strategies listed below to prepare for a sales call. The first three of these steps form the acronym PAL: "Bring your PAL (your Purpose/Agenda/Limit) to every meeting." PAL is a simple format that increases meeting productivity and direction.

1. Purpose—Define the reason for your meeting.

2. Agenda—Create a list of items to be discussed.

3. Limit your time—and how long your meeting will last.

4. Prepare questions in advance. Write questions down and choreograph them. Start with close-ended questions that only require one-word answers like yes or no, or very short and specific answers. Then add open-ended questions that require an opinion or more description. Develop a nice mix of open and closed-ended questions to create a conversation flow. (See more on questioning in Chapters 5 and 6.)

5. Listen. Questioning without listening is like selling without closing. Yet, listening is a skill that needs to be practiced to perfect. (See more on listening in Chapters 5 and 6.)

6. Involve the client by asking questions and effectively using silence to help further the sales process.

7. Prepare for objections. Seek them out if they do not come up in the conversation. By asking, "What might prevent you from going with us?" you will smoke out objections you may have otherwise missed. Preparing to receive objections builds confidence and furthers the sales process.

Top Ten Ways to Prepare for a Sales Call

1. **Purpose.** (Why are you meeting?)
2. **Agenda.** (What are the topics you will be discussing?)
3. **Limit.** (How long will you meet?)
4. **Questions.** (Prepare open-ended and closed-ended before meeting.)
5. **Listen.** (Keep reminding yourself to understand the prospect/customer interests and needs. Generate interest.)
6. **Involve every mind.** (Maintain campaign.)
7. **Objections.** (Expect and welcome them.)
8. **Close.** (Ask for the next-step commitment)
9. **Referrals.** (Ask who else could benefit?)
10. **Follow up.** (Keep all promises made.)

---

8. Prepare to close. Know when you plan on closing and rehearse what you will say. If you're not solidifying the deal, then don't always go

for the close of the deal; in many cases close to schedule the next step. (See more on closing in Chapters 5 and 6.)

9. Ask for referrals. When you ask, "Who else do you know that might be interested in utilizing our technology?" you will be able to link and leverage your business. (See more on referral requests in Chapter 4.)

10. Follow-up on all commitments and promises. Prepare for this by anticipating the promises you foresee being made (i.e., proposals drafted, research provided, etc.). Plan time after your meeting to follow through on those promises. (For more information on follow-up strategies, see Chapter 4.)

BOTTOM LINE **Prepare for Success**

When preparation meets opportunity, success is inevitable. Without preparation, results are strictly hit-or-miss.

KEY CONCEPT **EXPECTATION #6: BE A CUSTOMER-FOCUSED SELLER**

An old adage says that throughout the sales call the customer is thinking, "What's in it for me?" or "Why should I listen to you?"

Conducting each sales call with a customer-centered focus sounds simple and elementary. Yet, how many sales professionals really manage to do it?

Many sales professionals do a "data dump" in an attempt to hit hot buttons. A data dump usually goes like this: "We do this and this and this and also this. Isn't that great? So, what do you think?!" It is far better to frame questions to pinpoint a true need. Focusing in on the client's needs versus your interests is essential to effective selling. Once the client's true need is uncovered, then *and only then* can you determine the most appropriate information to share to further the relationship and the sale.

BOTTOM LINE **STAY CUSTOMER-FOCUSED**

Don't lose sight of the obvious: What's in this for the customer?

EXPECTATION #7: SINCERELY MAKE THE CLIENT FEEL IMPORTANT

Everyone likes to feel important and part of the process. If you focus on the details that matter to the client or acknowledge when the client makes impressive insights, you will strengthen your relationship. By giving compliments that are well warranted, you strengthen the bond between you and your client.

 IF YOU SAY IT, YOU HAD BETTER MEAN IT

Flattery without sincerity will get you nowhere. Sincere compliments will enhance relationships.

BOTTOM LINE **Mutual Respect Yields Greater Results**

People like to work with others who respect them and recognize their contributions. Making your client feel important in a genuine and sincere way will strengthen the bond between you.

 EXPECTATION #8: INTEGRITY

Integrity means adhering to a code of values—completeness, wholeness, uprightness—that is evidenced in character and action. Integrity involves thinking of yourself as a sales professional taking an active consultative interest in your client/prospect, versus being a salesperson who is selfishly just trying to close deals. In essence, this means focusing on developing a relationship-oriented partnership versus a take-the-money-and-run code of conduct.

When thinking of the true meaning of integrity, a quote from Emerson comes to mind: *"What you are speaks so loudly, I can't hear what you say."*

Out of all the expectations you set for yourself, integrity is the core where the truth is found.

Test for Integrity

Use this Integrity Profile as a self-management tool. Answer the following questions to create your personal character profile and integrity guide:

1. Who am I in the sales process?
2. What do I represent?
3. I would describe my character as follows . . .
4. Would I buy from me? Why/why not?
5. How am I different from the rest?
6. What value do I bring to the client?

BOTTOM **True Success Lies in True Value**

LINE The success that comes from having integrity is summed up well in a quote from Albert Einstein, who said, "*Let us not strive to be people of success, but let us strive to be people of value. If you are of value to your friends, clients, family and community you truly are a success.*"

YOU GET WHAT YOU EXPECT

The process of creating, defining, and adhering to expectations sets the standard for success. The eight expectations detailed in this chapter provide a starting point. So take a moment to jot down what you expect of yourself as a competent and successful self-managed sales professional. If you keep this list visible and review it daily, you will continue to evolve into a person of great integrity. Remember, you tend to get what you expect.

Self-Motivation

There comes a moment when you realize that anything is possible—
that nothing is too good to be true.

Kobi Yamada

The root of the word *motivation* is *motive,* which means to act. So in order to be self-motivated, you mainly need to determine those activities that you must focus on to act in a way that yields the best results. Inspiration is another factor that comes into play when determining motivational influences. Inspiration is an idea or influence that compels one to act.

Below are some strategies to help you awaken the peak performer within and unlock your own powerful self-motivation.

KEY CONCEPT — PEAK PERFORMANCE

What characteristics come to mind when you think of peak performance? Do you envision people who are highly successful? Those who beat the odds? People who stick with a vision until it becomes a reality? Persistent, take-charge individuals?

I used to have a talk show on CableVision entitled, "At Work with Joy Baldridge."® The focus of the show was interviewing the CEOs, presidents, and sales leaders of Fortune 500 companies. (Fortunately, in the Stamford, Connecticut, area, where I am located, there are more Fortune 500 headquarters than just about anywhere else in the country.) I thought that by interviewing the top people in top organizations I would be able to find some common traits that they possessed that I could share with others who desire to get to the top of their game. What I discovered was that most of the people I interviewed lived and worked by a specific set of principles. Some of the key principles are summarized in Table 2.1. You will also find them explained in more detail below: Compete against yourself. A true leader blazes the trail.

> Ruthlessly compete with your own best self.
> *Apollo Engineers*

TABLE 2.1 CORE PRINCIPLES OF HIGHLY SUCCESSFUL PEOPLE

Compete Against Yourself: Lead the Way by Improving Continuously on Your Personal Best

Benchmarking
Determine where you are versus where you want to be.

Cumulative Frequency
Do a little more each day to reach your goals.

Adaptability to Change
Expect change to occur—and embrace it.

Clear Vision
Know what you want and actually see it happening.

Flexibility
Be open-minded.

Continuous Education
Make consistent efforts to learn.

Self-Recognition
Say praise phrases to keep you going.

 BENCHMARKING

Benchmarking means determining where you are and where you want to be.

You can benchmark just about anything. Some examples of benchmarking include:

1. Determining how many active clients you currently have versus how many you would like to have

2. Calculating what your total sales revenue was last year versus what you want it to be this year

3. Analyzing the return on investment of time, energy, and revenue you made toward generating increased business versus what to keep or change moving forward.

Benchmarking is a critical self-management sales tool. It does not take very long to do and it adds essential focus to the selling process. When benchmarking, you remove yourself from the day-to-day activities that are all-consuming and get a quick glimpse of the bigger picture, and how to live it. A good question to ask yourself is, "What can I do from where I am with what I have to get what I want?"

 CUMULATIVE FREQUENCY

Most top executives agree, that doing a little more each day gradually over time is a highly effective way to become a peak performer. Whether you arrive at the office a little earlier, stay a little later, or carve out some time in your hectic day for yourself to think and form creative strategies, doing a little more each day with a solid intention of getting ahead really pays off. Many sales professionals get trapped into an all-or-nothing mindset. But by focusing on a few extra activities that can be done in your day, gradually over time, performance will soar. Some examples of gradual incremental gains are:

1. Write one extra thank-you note each week.

2. Make two extra sales cold calls each day.

3. Follow up on one additional pending client each day.

4. Read one brief article in a sales or marketing magazine every other day.

TABLE 2.2 MAKE THE COMMITMENT TO GET MORE DONE

- Write one extra thank-you note each week.
- Make two extra sales cold calls each day.
- Follow-up on one additional pending client each day.
- Read one brief article in *Sales and Marketing* magazine every other day.

Cumulatively speaking, these added activities done consistently over time, yield dramatic results. See Table 2.2.

Make Just One More Call . . .

Make one extra sales call a day, and watch your revenue stream increase steadily over time.

ADAPTABILITY TO CHANGE

"I learned to embrace change" is what Gaynor Kelley said when asked how he became CEO of Perkin Elmer after nearly 40 years of employment. Embracing change is a concept that sounds exciting, yet in reality it is not so easy to do because it is more comfortable to keep doing the same old thing. But there can be a problem with that, because if you always do what you have always done, you'll always get what you always got, which isn't good enough anymore. Also, in today's fast-changing times this does not always hold true. You can very well end up getting less than you got before because your competition is surging ahead of you. One definition of insanity is doing the same thing over and over again and expecting different results, whereas what most sales professionals don't realize is that resisting change is the real insanity. The formula for successful change is to change gradually over time. If you try something new, say for a period of 15 to 20 days, it can become a habit. So ask yourself, what changes do you want to make in the way you are running your business? How will you begin? How will you continue?

Before You Make Changes, Plan for Adjustments

When you decide to change the way you are currently conducting your business, think through all the pros and cons in advance, and give yourself enough time to adjust your plan if and when setbacks occur.

BOTTOM LINE — Change Can Be Awkward, Until You Get Used to It

Try doing a routine activity differently. Accept the awkward stage. Work through it, until you discover the true benefits of change.

If you fear change, leave it here.
Sign on a restaurant tip jar

CLEAR VISION

Clear vision is knowing what you want, and actually creating a picture in your mind of it happening. It is developing the ability of visualizing your future. To do this, peak performing sales professionals recommend carving out some downtime for visualization. Daily five- to ten-minute visualization sessions are ideal, but weekly and monthly sessions will also work. Many sales masters report that initially the thought of taking any downtime for visualizing was unconscionable! How could precious sales time be sacrificed for mere contemplation! No way! But those who made the conscious effort and steadfast commitment to change their ways were astonished at how much more productive, focused, and confident they became.

The concept of clear vision reminds me of Walt Disney. He was indeed the epitome of the classic visionary. His lifelong philosophy was, "*If you can dream it, you can do it!*" He set his sights on a keen vision to bring happiness and joy to children and adults alike. Recently, when I was visiting Walt Disney World, I happened to call guest services and heard a story I'll share with you.

Disney World in Orlando, Florida, was completed and opened to visitors in 1971. Unfortunately Walt had died before the grand opening. On opening day a reporter was interviewing Walt's brother Roy and said, "Isn't it a shame that your brother didn't live to see Disney World." Upon which Roy Disney replied, "I don't understand what you mean. Don't you see, he saw it . . . so you could see it."

Do you see it? Your future existence? Carve out some downtime today and dream it.

The greatest thing is, at any moment, to be willing to give up who we are in order to become all that we can become.

Max DePree

FLEXIBILITY

Being flexible starts with possibility thinking. It means to avoid locking in to only one method of doing things. One key to taking on a flexible attitude is to apply the reversal of thought concept by taking a thought like "I can't do it" and switching it to the more adaptable "How can I do it?"

No Excuses

Being flexible does not mean being lackadaisical or *laissez-faire.* Instead, you are simply seeking out creative ways of coping when you hit road-blocks. Rather than resisting doing something productive, switch your thinking to a "can-do" attitude.

CONTINUOUS EDUCATION

Are you finding ways to improve yourself on a continuous basis? Peak performers, in addition to setting day-to-day activity goals, also set self-development goals. An example would be planning to attend one sales-related seminar per quarter. Another would be to read one confidence-building article a day from *Success* magazine. By setting specific education-related goals, you are building positive momentum and valuable knowledge that will allow you to excel.

Take Time Out for Learning: for Both New and Review

Don't let the ball drop while fulfilling your mission of continuous growth. Plan ahead which courses you plan to take, register for them and block the time out on your calendar. Also, beware of the "been there, done that" syndrome. If the information you are receiving from magazines, books, or seminars is useful even though it may not be completely new to you, stick with it. Repetition is a powerful learning tool and should not be readily discounted as unimportant.

It's what we learn after we know it all that counts.
John Wooden

SELF-RECOGNITION

Self-recognition is a very important part of the formula for successful self-managed selling. It entails praising yourself for a job well done when no one else is there to "catch you doing something right." The reason self-recognition is so essential is because it spurs you on to more and greater accomplishments. This spontaneous personal feedback is one of the greatest motivators for self-managed sales professionals.

Self-recognition is sometimes easier said than done. You may take for granted some of your accomplishments. So, first of all, it is important to recognize your positive actions as they occur, then think of what you can say to yourself to feel good about what you have done. You have to really think through carefully which words you would choose to say to yourself. Focus in on those words that truly motivate you. Not everyone is motivated by the same words.

There are four types of sales personalities: (1) Those who seek overt praise and recognition such as, "You're amazing, great, and sensational!"; (2) those who get full satisfaction out of being helpful, reliable, and dedicated; (3) those who seek recognition and satisfaction based on beating the odds, crushing the competition (i.e., "winning"); and (4) those spurred on by recognition that is nurtured by providing the right solution, finding the perfect application to fulfill the customer's need.

Which of the following "praise phrases" work best for you? Say the following praise phrases to yourself and see which one makes you feel of value and importance. "You are amazing, brilliant, totally awesome!" . . . "You are tremendously dedicated and helpful!" . . . "You're #1!" (the best) . . . or "You are absolutely right!" (perfect). Or, perhaps, maybe a simple "Good job!" works best for you. The point is that although different people respond differently to various praise phrases, most salespeople are motivated by some sort of verbal praise. By telling yourself the praise phrase that gives you the best energy surge and positive reinforcement, you can expect to acquire even higher levels of confidence, energy, ability, self-esteem, and self-motivation.

NONVERBAL SELF-PRAISE

Nonverbal self-praise can work as well as verbal self-praise does. As corny as it may sound, physically giving yourself two pats on the back after an achievement can motivate you to continue to work with high energy and enthusiasm. I know, because I do it. At first it felt a little awkward to reach over and pat myself on the back. And in

TABLE 2.3 CLASSIC AND EFFECTIVE NONVERBAL SELF-PRAISE

- Two pats on the back
- Two pats on the back and a rub
- Touchdown victory gesture
- Thumbs up
- Two thumbs up

public I have to do it ever so covertly. But it really can escalate your energy level and create a positive attitude.

A friend of mine, upon discovering that I did the two-pat self-recognition technique, exclaimed that I was really missing out. I asked curiously, "Well, what do *you* do?!" He replied, "I do two pats . . . and a rub!" "Wow, I like that!" I said. And I've been adding the rub ever since.

In addition to the two pats, and two pats and a rub, there is a third nonverbal self-recognizer: thumbs up, or the double thumbs up meaning everything is going well. Another is making the touchdown sign by raising both arms in the air simultaneously signifying that you scored the sale, the appointment, and so forth. The point is that rewards, whether verbal or nonverbal, are an essential part of motivation. See Table 2.3 for some nonverbal praise ideas.

BOTTOM LINE When No One Is There to "Catch You Doing Something Right," Catch Yourself

Being a self-managed sales professional, you are responsible for providing adequate self-recognition, be it verbal or nonverbal. Use these techniques—and watch your sales soar!

KEY CONCEPT THE OGIVE CURVE®: PUTTING ERRATIC EMOTIONS IN CHECK

Understanding the concept of the Ogive Curve® helps put erratic emotions in check. The Ogive (pronounced *O-Jive*) Curve is a cumulative frequency Curve. What this definition means is that one point builds to the next, which builds to the next. The Ogive Curve is typically found in statistics. As you discover the way an Ogive Curve is formulated in this section you will see how significant this curve is to the sales process. (See Table 2.4.) Many people are unaware of the Ogive Curve and its strong correlation to ups and downs within sales cycles.

TABLE 2.4 HOW AN OGIVE CURVE WORKS (TAKING YOU FROM THE DEPTH OF THE CAVE TO THE HEIGHT OF THE WAVE!)

"The Cave"

Negative Ogive: You're in the doldrums. Down, down, down!
- (X) The sale that you thought you had just closed falls through.
- (X) A prospect cancels an appointment and decides not to reschedule.
- (X) You have to inform the client that the product you just sold him has a few technical glitches that you were unaware of.

"The Wave"

Positive Ogive: You're on a roll! Up, up, up!
- (X) Your commission check turns out to be $1,000 more than you expected!
- (X) A prospect returns your call and sounds interested in moving to the next step!
- (X) You win some unexpected business!

You have the power to modify and control the way that you view events by the way in which you build your mental structure.

When you get into a tight place and it seems that you can't go on, hold on, for that's just the place and time that the tide will turn.

Harriet Beecher Stowe

Basically, the sales process is nothing more than plots on an Ogive Curve. There are two types of Ogive: *positive* Ogive and *negative* Ogive. An example of positive Ogive is when one positive event occurs in your day (i.e., you win some unexpected business), then another positive thing occurs (a prospect returns your call and sounds interested in moving to the next step), followed by another positive occurrence (your commission turns out to be $1,000 more than you expected) . . . and you are on a roll! Have you ever had a day like that? Everything is going your way! You can do no wrong.

Therefore, positive Ogive is when one event is added to another, which is in turn added to another, and your day is going up, up, up. You have probably had days like this and have loved them. The only problem is that there is also negative Ogive. Negative Ogive is when one disappointment occurs (i.e., the sale you thought you just closed falls through), followed by another disappointment (a prospect cancels an appointment and decides not to reschedule), followed by another (you have to inform the client that the product you just sold has a few technology glitches you were unaware of). Do you find that just as positive Ogive happens cumulatively, so does negative Ogive?

Out of nowhere it seems that everything is falling apart. When negative Ogive occurs, it can get very depressing. The point is that it is important that you prepare ways to cope and keep things in perspective when the ups get very high and the downs get very low. If you internalize the lows of sales excessively, it can be very stressful and become counterproductive. Instead, if you use the Ogive Curve to keep track of what is happening in your day and plot the highs and lows on a graph, it allows you to avoid internalizing too much adversity, which in turn frees you from acquiring unnecessary negative emotion. Thus, instead of saying, "I'm having a bad day," replace that with the concept that there's a lot of negative Ogive going on and ask yourself, "What can I do to bring myself out of it?"

Also, the Ogive Curve allows you to be more aware of your self-perception of events that happen in your day. Is your perception of events increasingly positive or negative?

Ride the Wave, Avoid the Cave

When you are having a great (positive Ogive) day and you are on a roll, keep making sales calls and ride that "wave" as long as you can. When negative Ogive seeps in, don't get stuck in the negativity "cave." Recognize it and break free from it, and get back to positive Ogive.

KEY CONCEPT — MANAGING YOUR OGIVE

There are specific ways to manage your Ogive in order to allow you to feel in control of your emotions. The four main methods are: (1) self-talk—developing positive ways to talk to yourself; (2) flooding—repeating over and over again a positive expression or affirmation; (3) visible reminders—displaying inspiring quotes; and (4) happy file—maintaining a file of uplifting items.

Self-Talk

Self-talk is what you say when you talk to yourself. Unfortunately, some research has indicated that approximately 80 percent of what we say to ourselves on a daily basis tends to be negative. This is not necessarily because we are negative people, it's just that there is a good amount of negativity that comes at us, through the media, gossip, announcements regarding downsizing and plant closings, and so on.

The first step is in being aware of the fact that so many negative thoughts can occupy so much of your mind. You cannot prevent a negative thought from entering your mind, but you can control whether or not it stays there. Next, you need to generate expressions that you can say to counter the negativity. Your favorite praise phrases (discussed earlier in this chapter) can work well in countering negative thoughts.

I discovered one of my favorite expressions while reading *How to Think Like a Millionaire* by Mark Fisher and Marc Allen. In their book there was a story about a French pharmacist named Emile Coué. Coué became known for helping sick people become healthy and poor people become wealthy by having them recite to themselves an expression twenty times a day. That expression was as follows: *"Every day, in every way, I am getting better and better."* As simple as these words seem, their power when repeated over and over can exert a strong influence on positive self-perception. (Coué was also the inventor of the placebo concept; yet another example of mind over matter.)

If Coué's expression doesn't grab you, you may want to try one from Thoreau, who wrote, *"Walk with confidence in the direction of your dreams, act as though it were impossible to fail."*

When I was starting my own business as a sales consultant, I had to give up the secure perks of a steady base salary, predictable commission structure (from the account base I had established over the years), solid health benefits, and 401k plan. A friend, Mark Riesenberg, expert on the goal achievement process, suggested that I "flood" Thoreau's expression that I just shared with you with blind faith and "take the plunge." I have never had a moment of regret. I've been far too busy pursuing and actualizing my dreams. Which reminds me of another "flood-worthy" quote:

It's time to start living the life we've imagined.
Henry James

If you are still stumped as to what to say when you talk to yourself, you may want to pick up a copy of *The Self-Talk Solution* by Shad Helmstetter. You will find a wealth of flooding-type expressions to choose from.

Flooding

"Flooding" is the concept of repeating over and over again a positive expression or affirmation. By repeating a specific phrase, you strengthen your subconscious thinking process and begin to act with renewed confidence.

There is nothing good or bad, but thinking makes it so.
William Shakespeare

The Power of Flooding

Avoid underestimating (or overestimating) the power of flooding. If you believe it is too simple to work—or just the reverse, if you rely too heavily on its power—you could be setting yourself up for disappointment. Try flooding your most meaningful expression twenty times a day for several days and watch for gradual, and possibly dramatic improvements in your confidence, stamina, outlook, and success.

Visible Reminders

Keep motivational quotes, along with statements of your goals and dreams visible as part of your day-to-day environment—on your desk, on your bulletin board, on the side of your computer, etc. When information is written down and kept in a visible place, it becomes tangible. Many times your mind may fill itself up with some of the wildest notions. Have you ever thought too much about how you think a sale might be going? (Or not going?) Most people tend to move in the direction of their current most dominant thought. By having positive visual reminders around, you are more likely to find yourself unconsciously seeking out and enjoying success. The following quotes are motivational expressions that I've seen visibly displayed on the desk of sales reps.

They say you can't do it, but sometimes that doesn't always seem to work.
Casey Stengel

You miss 100 percent of the shots you never take.
Wayne Gretzky

When you have exhausted all possibilities, remember this—you haven't.
Thomas Edison

Others can stop you temporarily, only you can do it permanently.
Page Sullivan

If you are already walking on thin ice, why not dance?
Gil Atkinson

For every obstacle there is a solution over under around or through.
Dan Zandra

You have to think anyway, so why not think big?
Donald Trump

You'll see it, when you believe it.
unknown

No one has ever drowned in his own sweat.
D. H. Thomas

Act as if what you do makes a difference. It does.
William James

We relish news of our heroes, forgetting that we are extraordinary to someone too.
Helen Hayes

Do your work with your whole heart and you will succeed—there is so little competition.

Elbert Hubbard

Yesterday is history, tomorrow a mystery. Today is a gift, that's why they call it the present.

unknown

To know even one life has breathed easier because you have lived; that is to have succeeded.

Ralph Waldo Emerson

What wealth does is give one the freedom to choose how to spend one's day.

Richard Branson, Virgin Airlines

Money is not the most important thing in the world. Love is. Fortunately, I love money.

Jackie Mason

I have enough money to last me the rest of my life unless I buy something.

Jackie Mason

May happiness touch your life today as warmly as you have touched the lives of others.

Rebecca Forsythe

Begin doing what you want to do now. We are not living in eternity. We have only this moment sparkling like a star in our hand and melting like a snowflake.

Marie Beynon Ray

Don't Quit

When things go wrong as they sometimes will
When the road you're trudging seems all uphill
When the funds are low and the debts are high
And you want to smile, but have to sigh
When care is pressing you down a bit
Rest if you must but don't you quit
Success is failure turned inside out
The silver tint of the clouds of doubt
And you can never tell how close you are
It may be near when it seems so far
So stick to the fight when you're hardest hit
It's when things go wrong that you mustn't quit.

unknown

HAVE YOU REMINDED YOURSELF TODAY HOW TERRIFIC YOU ARE?

Self-Talk
Say positive words to yourself that make you feel good.

Flooding
Repeat your self-talk 20 to 30 times a day.

Visible Reminders
Keep motivational quotes, along with your goals and dreams, where you can see them.

Happy File
Create a file of notes, cards, and articles that make you happy and keep you inspired. Peruse your happy file from time to time.

Happy File®

A "happy file"® is a file folder filled with things that make you smile. Is your bulletin board overflowing with fun photos, personal notes, greeting cards, and inspirational quotes?

It may be time to create a happy file. Leave the visible reminders you need up and put the rest in your happy file. Keep your happy file somewhere easily accessible to look through from time-to-time, to remind you of good times supportive friends and great achievements. Your happy file thus becomes a positive Ogive Curve—one positive point accumulating with another, pushing you toward greater achievement. Giving you a positive perspective. A mindset that allows you to regroup your thoughts and start again fresh.

You may have a fresh start any moment you choose, for this thing we call "failure" is not the falling down, but the staying down.

Mary Pickford

 POWER WORDS®

Another way to manage your Ogive is with the concept of power words.® When you feel the negative Ogive seeping into your day, you must immediately do something to bring yourself out of it. Otherwise it will consume you.

A power word is a word or phrase that you say to yourself that makes you feel strong so you can deal with, or counter, the negative Ogive coming at you. It could be a word or phrase that is calming, energizing, rejuvenating, inspirational, hard-charging, or even sentimental. Some examples of power words created by top sales professionals are listed in the following paragraphs, along with the stories behind them. As you read through all the power words and their personalized meaning, start to formulate the words that work best for you.

Words That Can Change Your Outlook— Power Words

"Invincible"

One sales professional stated that the first word that came to mind when asked to think of a power word for himself was "invincible." What that word meant to him was unstoppable. The dictionary definition of invincible is: incapable of being conquered, overcome, or subdued.

Debbie Thomas, the famous Olympic figure skater, also selected "invincible" as her power word. When asked to write down on her application to Stanford University the one word she would choose to describe herself, she wrote *invincible!*

"Kryptonite"

Kryptonite is the first power word that I created for myself. I was making the transition from being an inside salesperson to an outside salesperson. I was so nervous, because though I felt fully comfortable on the phone, I was far less comfortable in person with prospects and customers. The only words I could say to myself when I went on sales calls were, "I'm so nervous, I'm so nervous!" Which, of course, made me even more nervous!

I knew I needed to get rid of that negative self-talk. So I started asking myself "What word will make me feel strong?" The word "strong" itself just didn't do it for me. So I thought, "What's incredibly strong?" Superman's strong. Steel is strong. The "man of steel" is stronger than anyone else on the planet. But, what's stronger than Superman? Ah-ha! . . . Kryptonite! Because Kryptonite weakens Superman!

After doing my homework I discovered that there are two types of Kryptonite, red and green. Since green is the color of money, which itself is very powerful, I wrote my Power Word, "KRYPTONITE," in bright green Magic Marker on a piece of paper and stuck it in a visible place in my briefcase. Thus, every time I opened my briefcase, I was instantly reminded of my potential strength. It still works as a confidence-booster for me.

"Hot Stuff"

One woman shared with me that she arrived at her power word years ago through her father. She was 16 at the time and about to start her first job, which was at a local McDonald's. Her father sat her down and said, "You are going to be serving customers who may at times be demanding and want their food fast. Now, if anyone ever gives you a hard time, you just remember that you're hot stuff! And to this day, "hot stuff" works for her.

"Relax"

Although this word hardly sounds like a word of power, in an indirect way, it can be. An advertising account executive in New York City repeats this word over and over to herself when traveling in taxis from one sales call to the next. She finds that it enables her to take a moment to catch her breath. Before she began repeating this power word, she always found herself stressed out and exhausted. After adopting it, she found that her energy was promptly renewed. Her thoughts became clearer, and her emotions, which used to go haywire, became more rational. Result: More self-control = more sales.

"Perspective"

One sales professional, upon learning the power word concept, exclaimed, "I can't think of just one word. It's all a matter of perspective." At which point he declared, "Ah-ha, *perspective* will be my power word. From that moment, the quality of his sales decisions improved due to his new focus on putting sales circumstances in perspective."

"Flipper"

Mary, a sales professional from Hawaii, was having a tough time dealing with difficult people she encountered on various sales calls. She tried to think of words that would help her avoid getting riled up when hard-charging negotiators aggressively tried to force a better deal or attacked the integrity of her product or service.

Mary was not one to readily buy into a concept like Power Words. Her initial impression was that it was pure "psychobabble." But, after a little thought, she came up with her own unique power word: "Flipper." "Flipper?" I asked. "What does that do for you?" "Well," she said, "Flipper reminds me of the dolphin on the 1960's TV show. A dolphin is a powerful and playful creature. It glides through the ocean so smoothly. Flipper is actually a silly word to say and the sound of it makes me laugh. Nevertheless, I think it is admirable that dolphins are stronger than sharks and other sea creatures, yet dolphins are smart enough to reserve using their awesome power unless it is absolutely necessary.

"I must admit that the first time I used this power word it seemed a bit strange," said Mary. "I was facing a person across the bargaining table who kept trying to use savvy intimidation tactics, while I kept reciting to myself: 'Flipper,' 'Flipper,' 'Flipper.' It seems absurd, yet in doing this, it instantly and drastically lowered my anxiety level and allowed me to psychologically thwart the aggressive advances that were being made. Figuratively speaking, I could visualize 'flipping' them aside, and addressing the core issues."

"Surrender"

Roger, a copier salesperson in Westchester County, New York said that his power word is surrender. When I asked him why he selected this word, he somewhat reluctantly confessed that he used to be a very pushy and obnoxious salesperson. He would be "all over" his prospects, trying every way possible to force his product upon them.

He found that applying "heavy pressure" sales tactics was not an effective or rewarding method of selling. Along the way, he started to take martial arts and discovered the power of the concept of surrendering. He decided to use the power word *surrender* while out in his territory. Instead of talking endlessly all about his copier and rushing to "the close," he would start to "surrender" by asking open-ended questions and actively listening. Surrendering his own needs and agenda and yielding to the customer's needs and agenda made a sudden and drastic impact in his sales success.

"Show Me the Money!"

When it comes right down to it, many sales professionals take on the Jerry McGuire philosophy of

"Show me the money!" They are in it for the fun, the challenge, and most of all the personal and financial rewards.

Another power phrase—"Just do it!"—comes up quite often. This says it all—no room for excuses.

KEY CONCEPT   POISON WORDS®

"Poison words"® are words that can inhibit progress. They are words and phrases that get in the way of success. Some classic poison words are *could, would,* and *should.* Unless you are using these words for creative brainstorming exercises to troubleshoot or to generate new ideas, they can definitely interfere with your success.

The simple statement, "I really should make more cold calls each week," can produce negative feelings of regret, guilt, and worry that can rob your energy and defeat your spirit. If, instead, you say, "I'll organize my database so that I can make five cold calls a day in addition to my follow-up calls and company visits," you will probably avoid negative baggage and be much better off.

Other poison words are *but, try, can't,* and *if only.* Here are some examples of how damaging these words can be:

"But"—"I want to break into that new account, but the competition seems to have it locked." The problem with "but" is that it creates a defeatist attitude.

"Try"—"I'll try to get back to you on that." The problem with "try" is that it acts as an excuse. It gives you an out. It is a statement that lacks confidence and certainty. "Try" does not reflect or imply decisive action. You either do it or you don't do it. There is no "try." Frequent use—or any use—of "try" in selling can be counterproductive, waffling and tearing down confidence. Therefore, don't "try" to avoid using "try"; simply omit try from now on.

"Can't"—If you think you can or you think you can't, you're right! "Can-do" always works better in increasing sales than "no-can-do."

> Whether you think you can or you can't, you're right.
>
> *unknown*

"If Only"—"If only I had formal sales training." "If only I had more experience." The problem with "if only" is that it promotes whining and can become self-defeating. There is an old adage, "If only pigs had wings, pigs could fly."

The saddest words of tongue or pen are these four words—it might have been.
Oliver Wendell Holmes

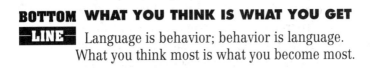

Watch Usage and Intent of Words

Not all poison words are necessarily bad. It's their usage and intent that matter most. Some people actually think of the word "try" as a power word (i.e., "I'll try my best!"). Yet, the phrase, "I'll do my best," conveys more confidence and can have more positive impact.

BOTTOM LINE WHAT YOU THINK IS WHAT YOU GET

Language is behavior; behavior is language. What you think most is what you become most.

It is not who we are that holds us back, it's who we think we're not.
Michael Nolan

FOR AN EMOTIONAL RESCUE, USE SELF-PRAISE

Many sales professionals seek recognition from external influences, such as clients, peers, and managers, but once you acquire the ability to praise yourself for a job well done you will be more in control of the way you manage your emotions as you experience the ups and downs of sales.

Time Management

"Be assured that you'll always have time for the things you put first."
Liane Steele

Would you agree that there just never seems to be enough time in a day to accomplish everything you need to do?

Of course many people in a variety of professions feel that way. The difference in sales is how dramatically the use of time affects the bottom line. Mismanagement of time can domino into lost opportunity of revenue. As a recruiter of sales professionals for over a decade, I discovered something in interviews about the time management traits of the superstars versus the rest.

Top producers would think of time in terms of seconds and minutes, whereas average salespeople would think in terms of hours and days. Every second counts in sales because there is and always will be (1) someone in great need of your product; (2) the competition fast on the trail; (3) a company becoming increasingly dissatisfied with their current vendor; and (4) new technology your company has created that will blow the competition away.

MANAGE TIME IN TERMS OF SECONDS AND MINUTES VERSUS HOURS AND DAYS

Manage time in terms of seconds and minutes. Thinking in smaller increments creates a greater sense of urgency to make a plan and rapidly implement it. It also becomes a motivational tool to encourage salespeople to keep going. It can almost become a game where you set target goals and race to achieve them. Therefore, the four benefits of managing time in small increments are that doing so (1) creates a greater sense of urgency, (2) heightens productivity, (3) increases motivation, and (4) crystallizes goals.

A goal is a dream with a deadline.

unknown

 SELF-QUESTIONING

Time is the sales professional's most precious resource. When it is used up it can never be retrieved again. It's gone. Yet so many salespeople mismanage their time. Some ways of time mismanagement are listed in Table 3.1.

One of the most effective techniques in time management is self-questioning. Self-questioning involves asking yourself specific questions about how you use your time. This technique demonstrates the epitome of self-management. It allows for more awareness and control over time and can be used as a self-discipline tool. Table 3.2 offers some sample self-questions about time management. Answering these questions will reveal whether you're using your time well or poorly. If you're not working on the right project (i.e., making the best use of your time), you need to command yourself to stop.

Self-discipline and staying on track with your sales goals comes from evaluating what activity you're doing and determining whether it makes sense to continue or if another activity will yield better results. Table 3.3 lists some self-discipline command phrases.

TABLE 3.1 MISMANAGEMENT OF TIME

- Perfection versus acceptable letter writing
- Unqualified target list
- Scheduling sales calls ineffectively
- Mailing information (slow) versus meeting (fast)
- Spending longer than necessary on client rapport-building
- Personal calls

TABLE 3.2 SAMPLE SELF-QUESTIONS

- Is this the best use of my time right now?
- What is the best use of my time right now?
- Is this activity bringing me closer to or farther away from my next customer?
- The next dollar? How profitable is that dollar?
- Is this task urgent?
- Is this task important?
- What obstacles am I creating by procrastinating?

The self-question method is particularly effective when used with the urgent/important model Stephen Covey made famous in his book *The 7 Habits of Highly Effective People: Powerful Lessons in Personal Change.* Covey wrote about a grid pertaining to what is urgent versus what is important. There are four categories in this grid: Quadrant 1, urgent and important, a crisis; Quadrant 2, not urgent but important, a proactive state; Quadrant 3, urgent but not important; and Quadrant 4, not urgent and not important.

Once aware of the four different quadrants you can be in, it is critical to determine what is the best use of your time by placing greater value on the important and urgent activities. Examples:

- If it's urgent and it's important, do it now. It is a crisis.

- If it is not yet urgent, but important, find time for some of these to-dos because working on them ahead of schedule will put you in a highly proactive state.

- If it is urgent but not important, who else can do it?

- If it is not urgent and not important, then why are you doing it?

Work expands so as to fill the time available for its completion.
Northcote Parkinson

TABLE 3.3 SELF-DISCIPLINE COMMAND PHRASES

- Stop, stop! I am commanding myself to stop.
- Write the activity I'm stopping on my "to-do list," to remember to do it later.
- Shift focus on what is most important and most urgent—the best use of my time right now.

TIME-WASTERS

The top six time-wasters in Corporate America are listed in Table 3.4. Let's conquer each of these time wasters one by one.

 START WITH THE LARGER TASKS FIRST

It is usually best to start with the largest task first, and break it down.

> Nothing is particularly hard if you divide it into small jobs.
> *Henry Ford*

 **TIME ROBBER #1: INTERRUPTIONS**

Typically the biggest time robbers are interruptions. Most people do not realize that there are many different types of interruptions. Table 3.5 lists the most common types of interruptions. Let's take each form of interruption and provide tips on how to deal with it.

Drop-In Visitors

In the office, drop-in visitors are people who stop by your desk to ask a question, discuss an idea, or shoot the breeze. They typically come in unannounced and seem to have little regard for protecting your precious time resource.

At your home office, a drop-in visitor could be the UPS or Federal Express person, the paperboy collecting subscription money, or a neighbor gathering signatures for a petition.

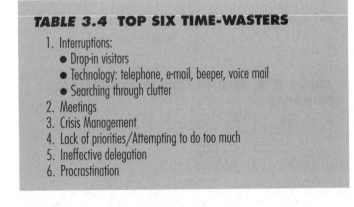

TABLE 3.4 TOP SIX TIME-WASTERS

1. Interruptions:
   - Drop-in visitors
   - Technology: telephone, e-mail, beeper, voice mail
   - Searching through clutter
2. Meetings
3. Crisis Management
4. Lack of priorities/Attempting to do too much
5. Ineffective delegation
6. Procrastination

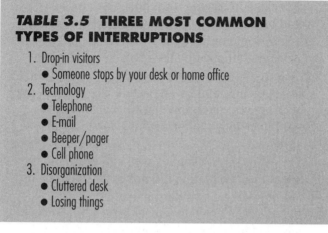

TABLE 3.5 THREE MOST COMMON TYPES OF INTERRUPTIONS

1. Drop-in visitors
   - Someone stops by your desk or home office
2. Technology
   - Telephone
   - E-mail
   - Beeper/pager
   - Cell phone
3. Disorganization
   - Cluttered desk
   - Losing things

In essence, a drop-in visitor is someone taking you away from something you need to be doing to get you closer to your goals. Each drop-in visitor claims that it will only take a minute, when you know far too well that there is nothing further from the truth.

If you don't have anything to do, don't do it here.

anonymous

The Plus, Plus, Dash®

One way to minimize interruptions (whether in person or telephone) while still making the person interrupting feel important (remember Expectation #7 in Chapter 1) is to practice a method called the "plus, plus, dash."®

I discovered the plus, plus, dash when I called my best friend at work. At the time Mary was the art director of a magazine and under a tremendously tight deadline. When I called, she said, "I'm really glad you called, and I really want to talk to you. I'm under a tight deadline; can I call you back in an hour?"

I said "Sure," and hung up. Then I thought, wait a minute. I'm not speaking to Mary, which was my purpose for calling, but I feel good. What did she do? As I traced back the elements of the conversation in my mind I realized that she had made two positive comments (which I labeled the plus, plus) and then she dashed off. From this encounter the term plus, plus, dash was created.

I decided to use the plus, plus, dash to see if it would help me save time when I received drop-in or telephone interruptions.

A vendor stopped by the office to ask how the new software was working. I said, "I'm really glad you stopped by, and I want to talk to you about my new program. Right now I'm working on a proposal I have to get out; can you give me a call tomorrow?"

On paper this all sounds well and good, but in reality the conversation did not go as smoothly as I had hoped. I was stuttering over my words. Why? Because I couldn't be sincere. I was not really glad he stopped by, and I didn't really want to speak to him. I realized I needed to practice the plus, plus, dash a little more.

Luckily, that night I received a telephone interruption during dinner. It was a long-distance telephone carrier calling. (Do you ever receive telephone interruptions during dinner?) Does he ever call you? He calls me all the time. I decided that I would try the plus, plus, dash again, this time focusing on sincerity.

The telemarketer said, "This is Dale in Dallas, Texas. How are y'all doing tonight?" I said, "Fine, Dale, and how are you?" "Great!" he said. Then I proceeded with sincerity by saying, "I'm really glad you called." (Plus.) He said, "You are?" And I said, "Yes, and I really want to speak with you." (Plus.) Upon which he replied, "You do?" And I said, "Yes, because I just signed up with another carrier, and I wanted to ask you to take me off your list, please." He honored the request.

What the plus, plus, dash does is provide a formula to divert interruptions to times when you can afford to have them. If an interruption occurs at a time that is less inconvenient than any other time then it is best to go ahead and handle it.

Keep in mind by using the plus, plus, dash method you become less of a victim and more in control of where your time is spent. Also, sometimes when you divert to a later time to speak, the person who came to you finds other ways to get his or her question answered.

It takes practice to perfect the plus, plus, dash. But once you get it down you will save a lot more time. Sales reps who have used the plus plus dash effectively have found it saves them one to two hours of time a day.

DANGER! **Watch Usage**

There are a few dangers you need to be aware of when making the decision to use the plus, plus, dash. First, don't use it every time. Obviously, there are some interruptions, crises, for example, that you'll need to attend to.

Also, play around with the wording of the plus, plus, dash to make it sound natural to you. For instance, "I'm really glad you called," might be a little too enthusiastic for you. Instead you may want to replace it with, "Thank you for calling, I'd like to help you with this . . . Right now, I'm tied up. Can we go over it first thing in the morning?"

Or, you could delegate the "dash" by saying, "Thanks for calling, that's an interesting request. I think Joe would probably have a little better insight to that than I would." (Again, sincerity is the key. You actually have to believe that Joe is an excellent resource to "dash" to.)

TiP **No "Buts" about It**

Be careful to avoid saying the word "but" when using the plus, plus, dash (i.e., "I'm glad you called, and I'd like to help *but* . . .") because the word *but* is known for acting like an eraser. It erases all the nice positive phrases you've used, and it emphasizes the dash. Some ask, "What can I use instead of *but?*" "*However,* perhaps?" Well, *however* has been described as a *but* in a tuxedo. The transitional phrase that seems to work best is "right now" (i.e., "Right now I'm in a meeting. Can we talk at 4:00 P.M.?").

The plus, plus, dash is a time management tool that will help you feel more in control of interruptions. It allows you more often than not to defer them to a more convenient time when you are less harried and have better focus, as opposed to "anytime" they arise. Once this skill is perfected, you will feel more confident in the way you handle interruptions and take charge of how you manage your time.

TiP **Stand Up and Save Time**

Another tip for handling an interruption by a drop-in visitor is to stand up and talk. It's called a "stand-up" meeting. People speak twenty percent quicker and listen more intently when having a stand-up meeting versus a sit-down discussion.

Avoid Abruptness

You have to be careful not to be too abrupt when you stand up or it may be perceived as awkward or threatening. It has to be done casually by moving gradually.

Walk with Me

You could also have a "walk-with-me" meeting. What this entails is indicating that you were just about to get a cup of coffee and you'd like to talk as you head over to the coffee machine. Upon reaching the coffee, go over practical solutions, confirm they are the solutions the person was looking for, and then go back to your desk, *alone*. The "walk-with-me" meeting prevents you from becoming a sitting duck in your office. People tend to stay much more time than necessary when they take a seat in your office.

Vary Your Approach

You have to vary your approach. You can't have a walk-with-me meeting every time someone drops by to talk. Use it as one of many ways to keep in control of your time.

Go to a Distraction-Free Zone

Along the lines of the walk-with-me meeting, the "distraction-free" meeting is another way to handle interruptions efficiently. When someone comes into your office to discuss something, say "I want to give this my full attention. Let's go into the conference room real quick." Go to the conference room. Set a time parameter. Focus on the issue at hand. Discuss it. Get agreement to action steps, and go back to your office—*alone*.

The whole point, once again, is that it is easier to focus when you are away from office distractions. Second, you solve problems more quickly when no distractions interfere, and third, the drop-in visitor is not hanging around your office for extended periods of time. Also, this technique acts as a way to make the drop-in visitor feel important because you are focusing solely on his or her issue without being distracted.

Remove All Chairs

A more drastic measure to ward off drop-in visitors is to eliminate all of the chairs from your office (except your own).

Some have tried to put piles of paper or boxes on chairs—only to find the drop-in visitor pick up the papers, put them on the floor, or their lap, and sit down anyway.

Be Flexible

It is important to remind yourself to be flexible, because throughout your day you will encounter numerous interruptions that can prevent things from getting done. Otherwise you may wind up pulling your hair out in utter frustration. Your ability to deal with these interruptions in a proactive manner is critical to your physical and mental well-being. Use the tips listed here, as needed, and they will assist you in recapturing otherwise lost time due to mismanaged interruptions. Use Table 3.6 as a reminder list.

TECHNOLOGY INTERRUPTIONS

This category used to be chiefly about telephone interruptions, but recent advances in technology have made e-mail, beepers/pagers, and cellular phones additional sources of interruptions. Keep in mind that the plus, plus, dash concept can also be applied to telephone, e-mail, and cell phones.

In addition to the plus, plus, dash, there are other ways to handle technology interruptions. They are detailed in the following paragraphs.

TABLE 3.6 TIPS FOR HANDLING DROP-IN VISITOR INTERRUPTIONS

- Plus, Plus, Dash
- Stand Up
- Walk and Talk
- Get Away
- Eliminate Chairs
- Formulate Courtesy

TELEPHONE INTERRUPTIONS:
SEVEN TIPS AND TWO DANGERS

Phone Zones

Creating "phone zones" helps. A phone zone is when you set a designated time segment for receiving calls. You simply ask people to contact you within a specific time frame. Most will comply and call back when you request. This saves you from playing phone tag or from receiving calls at inopportune times.

Give Yourself Time

When you ask someone to call you between 2:00 and 4:00 p.m., it seems most people tend to call close to or at 4:00. So, allow an extra half hour after the designated phone time for these last-minute callers. That way you still have time to talk without pressure or rushing.

Telephone Etiquette

Avoid saying "I'm waiting for an important call" or "I thought you were somebody else." It goes against your "make the caller feel important" expectation.

Caller ID

Caller ID is a very useful tool in minimizing telephone interruptions. It helps you to focus on those calls that are in line with your mission of the day, and those that seem to be the best use of your time.

If you do not have Caller ID, but do have an assistant, ask your assistant to tell you who is calling and why, to help further temper interruptions. Even though the assistant's message is an "interruption," you still are in control of how you will handle it.

Phone Placement

Putting the telephone in the right place on your desk allows for more efficient flow and for interruptions to be handled more smoothly. If you are right-handed, it is easier to have your phone on your left, so that you can pick up the receiver with your left hand, freeing your right hand for writing. (Reverse this tip if you are left-handed.) Also, headsets can make interruptions slightly less distracting, again because they enhance flow. It's less hectic dealing with the phone cord and receiver. While phone placement may seem like a minor detail, inefficiency here can add up to a lot of stressors that chip away at you throughout your day.

Four-Minute Courtesy Time

Place an hourglass with four minutes' worth of time on your desk. When your free time is limited but someone you need to speak with calls, turn over the hourglass. Have an in-depth and meaningful conversation as the sand sifts through the funnel. Once all the sand has gone through, you can ease into the plus, plus, dash with words such as "It was so great catching up with you. Thank you for keeping me posted. Speak with you next week to follow up."

Some sales professionals spend more time than necessary building rapport. In doing so, they are not only using up too much of their own precious time resources, but also using too much of their client's time as well. By keeping an eye on where the time is going, you will be able to build strong rapport in less time. This will allow you both to have more time in the day to focus on your goals. By being more time-conscious, you give "the gift of time" to both yourself and others.

The four-minute courtesy time can also be monitored by other methods. Two that come to mind are (1) look at your watch, and keep tabs on the time; and (2) use a call-timing device on your phone, if one is available. Time awareness helps in saving time.

"Can I Get Back to You on That, Please?"

The phrase "Can I get back to you on that please?" or the more assertive, "Let me get back to you on that," is an important one to know, because many times callers are looking for information or an answer from you, or to request a favor. You are in a very dangerous position if someone calls for a request and catches you in. Why? Because you can be caught off-guard. If you answer immediately, you may later regret what you said because you were unprepared to respond. The phrase, "I'll get back to you" gives you time to think before making a decision. It is a valuable phrase to have ready when answering your phone. Just think of all the times that you later regretted saying "yes" to unexpected called-in requests.

Wait a Minute

As mentioned before, you cannot always say you'll get back to someone. If you feel the caller will be annoyed by the possibility of endless phone tag if you say you'll get back to him or her, ask to put that person on hold for a minute. Think through all the ramifications if you honor their request and then respond. At least this gives you a little more time to formulate your answer.

When striving to be more time-efficient regarding dealing with telephone interruptions, keep Table 3.7 in mind.

Dealing with E-Mail Interruptions

E-mail is a constant interruption. Especially if you, like most people, have your system programmed to notify you every time an e-mail arrives. "Bing, bing, bing." If you are trying to create or perfect a document, the e-mail interruptions can be a major distraction. How do you cope? Here are a few tips to help.

- Deactivate your e-mail notification, so it won't jeopardize your communication flow, especially if you need to focus on a search or document for an extended period of time.

- Program your e-mail notification system to bing "when you have mail," but at a specified time interval, every 45 minutes or every 2 hours, for instance.

TABLE 3.7 SEVEN SUREFIRE WAYS TO HANDLE TELEPHONE INTERRUPTIONS

1. Plus, Plus, Dash: Say two positive remarks before dashing off
2. Phone Zones: Designate a specific uninterrupted time to bang out your calls
3. Etiquette: Make the caller feel important
4. Caller ID: See who's calling and decide the priority
5. Phone Placement/Headset: Add "flow" to your work environment
6. Four-Minute Courtesy: Take four minutes for quality time
7. "Let Me Get Back to You": Take a moment before impulsively answering called-in requests

- Turn the volume of your computer down to zero to eliminate the "bing."

- Ward off your curiosity by saving all unread e-mail for a time when you are done with your project and other urgent or important work. Then read and respond to all of the messages at once (unless you are waiting for a critical e-mail, of course). Many sales professionals find that when they tend to their e-mail each time a message arrives, they end up sorting through a lot of junk mail, and wasting precious time and momentum in the process.

Handling Beeper, Pager, and Cellular Phone Interruptions

Interruptions act as distractions. They take you away from your focus. They cause you to lose momentum. Beepers, pagers, and cell phones are necessary communication devices to keep you closely connected to your customer and the sale. However, they can be perceived as an annoying distraction when they go off in a meeting. Remember to shift to the vibrator mode, or leave these tools behind, when interacting with a client.

Clutter

Do you have a clutter pile? You know, a stack of papers on your desk in front of you or on the side of you where you put all the papers that you're not working on? Clutter in your office is often referred to as the "silent interruption." It is called this because as it lies on and around your desk it silently screams at you all day long to work on the pieces of the pile.

Clutter piles are stress sources. They rob your energy and divert your attention. The solution: Find a drawer in your desk or a space in your credenza to put your pile. That way it will be in a place from which you can retrieve necessary information but away from view so as to not distract you from focusing on your goals.

The remedies for handling clutter are listed in Table 3.8.

⬦DANGER!⬦ Out of Sight, Out of Mind

If you followed the previous advice, your pile is now out of sight. You may, therefore, be con-

TABLE 3.8 SIX WAYS TO CONQUER CLUTTER

- Remove it (most effective).
- Act on it.
- Toss it.
- Delegate it.
- File it.
- Ignore it (least effective).

cerned that you will forget to do something important that is in your pile. You may feel compelled to just do it now to get it out of the way. This is a mistake if it is not "the best use of your time." Instead, go through your pile and add the most urgent and important items, along with their necessary completion dates, to your to-do list. That way you won't forget them and will not fall victim to the concept of "out of sight, out of mind." A key element to this technique is that you must be in the habit of reviewing your to-do list frequently.

"I'll Just Take a Minute to Clean My Desk"

Cleaning your desk may take longer than you think. If you decide to complete each task on your

"Let me make a little note of that. I never seem to get anything done around here unless I make little notes."

desk as you clean, you may never finish. Most desks have an average of 36 hours of work on them. The better method, as mentioned on the previous page, is to find a place for your piles, this will keep your desk clear as well as your mind.

⬥KEY⬥ INTERRUPTION RECOVERY
CONCEPT

The reason interruptions are the number-one time robbers in corporate America today is not only due to the interruptions themselves, but because it takes time to recover from every interruption. The statistics are alarming. For each interruption that you encounter in your day, it takes an average of 2 to 15 minutes to recover, if you ever recover at all!

Two interruption recovery methods that have been proven to be effective are:

1. Making a mental or written note.
2. Using the red ruler method.

Now think about how many times drop-in visitors, voice mail, e-mail, and/or clutter interrupt you each day. Multiply that number by 2 to 15 minutes and you'll realize why you feel like you are constantly running out of time. Have you ever said to yourself at the end of the day, "I feel like I've gotten absolutely nothing accomplished"? It's usually a result of your time being stolen away, bit by bit, by interruptions.

> Time is a thief.
> *William Shakespeare*

Let's explore the two interruption recovery methods and discover how to gain more control over your day.

The Mental/Written Note

Recovery time after interruptions is reduced when a person immediately makes a mental or written note of what he or she was doing when the interruption took place. This technique enables you, after dealing with an interruption, to immediately recall what you were doing before it occurred, thereby allowing you to instantly regain your focus. By using this strategy, it takes only 2 to 15 seconds (versus 2 to 15 minutes) for you to recover. This substantial cumulative time-saver allows you more control over your day.

The Red Ruler Method

A second way to recover from interruptions is to use the "red ruler method." This technique involves having a red ruler (or any object of substantial visibility) on your desk. When an interruption occurs, slap the red ruler (or bright object) on top of the project you have been working on. Once the interruption has been resolved, look for the red ruler to recall where you were, and proceed on with the task. This technique also reduces interruption recovery time to 2 to 15 seconds per interruption.

Losing Things

Do you realize that (according to *Ripley's Believe It or Not*) the average person spends *six months* to *one year* of his or her life looking for misplaced objects?

Have you ever been working on a project, been distracted by an interruption (perhaps someone requesting that you send them a fax), and upon returning to your desk, discovered that the project was gone? Did it seem like it vanished right before your eyes!? At this point, you probably thought to yourself in disbelief, "What happened? Where is it? Who took it?" Then, before you start running around and accusing people of taking it, you say to yourself, "Wait a minute, let me retrace my steps."

Finally, after a painful search, "Eureka!" you find the project sitting next to the fax machine, where you accidentally left it. This happens all the time. How do you cope? Again, by applying the Mental/Written Note/Red Ruler concepts: Either tell yourself where you're putting something before you put it there, or mark your place with an object, like a red ruler. In doing so, you will lose fewer important papers and recover more effectively from the interruptions.

BOTTOM LINE **HAVE RECOVERY SYSTEMS**
Interruptions—drop-in visitors, e-mail, voice mail, and other cutting-edge technological inter-

ruptions, as well as excessive clutter—can rob tremendous amounts of time from your day. Having recovery systems in place will allow you to reclaim that time and focus it toward increased sales and productivity.

TIME ROBBER #2: MEETINGS

Meetings are the number-two time robber in organizations today, second only to interruptions. There are two main types of meetings:

Meetings You Lead

When you lead a meeting it is critical to follow specific guidelines that will allow you to get your message across in the most efficient and effective way.

To do so you will need an agenda, preferably in writing and sent ahead of time to those who will be attending your meeting.

Productive meetings stay on course. Any request to deviate from the meeting topic should be put on a flipchart or piece of paper with a promise to discuss it in the next meeting.

It is important to keep your meetings brief. If you are prepared and organized, you can most likely cover your agenda in 30 minutes, which is the optimal amount of time to run a meeting.

Have not only a start time, but also an end time to your meetings in order to make them more productive. The key (and challenge) is to stick to the time frame you give. Within this time frame it is essential to include an overview, your core message with examples, a question-and-answer period, a summary, and a commitment from the attendees to act on the concepts presented.

Few will complain about a meeting that ends early. Show you are a true leader and highly organized by ending on time or early.

Meetings You Attend

When attending a meeting it is best to arrive a little early. As Shakespeare said, *"Better three hours too soon, than a minute too late."* Although this quote is a bit excessive you get the idea. It is rude and selfish to enter a meeting late. Despite the fact that no one else seems to come on time, the fact that you do shows you care, that you're responsible and it makes you look good.

There are essential things that you will need to bring to a meeting you attend. Things such as the memo announcing the meeting, any work you've done for this meeting, your daily planner in case a follow-up meeting is scheduled or time sensitive commitments are made, a notepad, and reading material or other work you need to get done in case the meeting is delayed.

Always factor in extra time in your schedule in case the meeting runs over. Most meetings do run long, so expect it and prepare for it.

Write down all action steps that are necessary for you to take as a result of this meeting. Then block off a time line in your calendar to keep you on or ahead of schedule in completing these tasks. And finally, put action steps on your to-do list to ensure they get done!

See Tables 3.9 and 3.10 for reminders regarding meetings.

KEY CONCEPT — TIME ROBBER #3: CRISIS MANAGEMENT

Most business is crisis-driven today. Many salespeople find themselves spending the majority of their day putting out fires instead of sticking to their plan. (Would you agree that there are a lot of arsonists out there?)

The key in the real world is to do both. Put out the fires, if you cannot find someone else who can do that for you, and then have a solid plan to

TABLE 3.9 "MUST-HAVE"s FOR CONDUCTING MEETINGS

The meetings you lead must:
- Have an agenda (in writing and preferably sent in advance to attendees)
- Have a start and an end time
- Be limited to 30 minutes if possible
- Stick to the agenda
- Have a Q & A time
- Have a summary of meeting topics
- Summarize action steps
- Gain commitment among stakeholders
- Adjourn on time or early

TABLE 3.10 "MUST-DO"s FOR ATTENDING MEETINGS

For the meetings you attend, you should:
- Arrive early or on time
- Bring pertinent information
- Bring additional reading material or work in case of delay
- Bring notepad and pen
- Factor in extra time in your schedule for meeting running overtime
- Draw up questions to ask in Q & A
- Take notes
- Bullet action steps to take after the meeting
- Block deadlines off in calendar/planner

return to once the fire has been extinguished. Many sales professionals are excellent at putting out fires, but then once the fire is out, find themselves looking for the next fire to battle instead of going back to work on their plan.

One way to get back to your plan is to use the self-questioning technique mentioned earlier in this chapter. Ask yourself "What is the best use of my time right now?" Then answer the question and do it!

You will find the answer to this question on your to-do list, in your gut, or in your mind. Once you determine the answer, act on it.

This will help you to balance the amount of time you spend in your day on action versus reaction. It will allow you to manage crises more rationally and calmly and get more done in your day.

KEY CONCEPT — **TIME ROBBER #4: FAILING TO PRIORITIZE AND ATTEMPTING TO DO TOO MUCH**

Have you ever felt overwhelmed by all of the work you had to accomplish? Has this overwhelming feeling ever led to paralysis, where you had so much to do that you couldn't even begin to think where to start—and therefore you couldn't do *anything*?!

Fortunately, this frozen moment tends to be temporary. What usually gets sales professionals back on track is their "to-do" lists. Many sales professionals have to-do lists, but unfortunately many fail to commit them to writing or use them correctly. Most don't realize that there really are three specific forms of the proverbial to-do list. These are as follows:

Activity Lists (To-Dos)

Activity lists are the most popular ones and are considered to be the traditional "to-do" list. The mistake most people make is that they mix in their to-dos with goals and ideas. The problem with this is that you cannot "do" a goal. You can only do an activity that will lead you toward achieving your goal. Therefore, an activity is a definite to-do item—an action that you can take. It is *not* a goal or an idea. Goals and ideas need to be written on their own separate lists. They are described below. For specific guidelines on writing effective activity lists, see Table 3.11.

Goal Lists (Objectives)

A "goal list" is a list of objectives or projects that need to be accomplished within a certain time frame. As already mentioned, you cannot "do" a goal or an objective. What you can "do" is break down a goal into action steps. Since many sales professionals make the mistake of putting goals (thinking that they are activities) on their to-do list, they find that these items never get crossed off, and frustration sets in. This leads to a lack of accomplishment that deflates motivation.

The correct way to create a goal list is to brainstorm and write down all of the projects, goals,

---

TABLE 3.11 TWELVE TRAITS OF A HIGHLY PRODUCTIVE TO-DO LIST

1. Number each to-do item.
2. Start each item with an action verb (i.e., "Call Joann Smith").
3. Include complete information (i.e., phone number, fax #, purpose of call).
4. Each item is action-oriented—a "to-do," versus a goal or idea.
5. First write and number your list, then prioritize it.
6. Put all to-dos on one list in one place (computer or hand-written).
7. Write personal and business to-dos on the same list.
8. Write to-do lists preferably at the same time each day.
9. Do not rewrite entire to-do list each day; instead, carry forward key to-dos.
10. Review current and past to-do lists several times each day.
11. Cross off items that are done and say "Yes!"
12. Write deadlines and backup deadlines next to to-dos.

and objectives. Once the goal list has been created, action steps with deadlines must be determined and placed on activity lists. To-do lists are then created from action steps necessary to complete the projects.

Idea Lists (Thoughts)

Thoughts are powerful. Take time to dream. Think about how to penetrate more accounts, and how to link and leverage existing business. Then turn your dreams into reality by writing them down. In essence, put think to ink.

Capture your thoughts on your idea list, then transform them into goals. Break those goals down into to-dos, and you will differentiate yourself from all the rest!

In his classic book, *Think and Grow Rich,* Napolean Hill advises you to capture your ideas, because they are fleeting. Those who make the effort to capture their ideas and then to focus and act on them, gain the greatest success.

Always Be Prepared

Have you ever noticed that you get some of your greatest ideas at moments when you are unprepared to capture them? While in the shower, jogging, or falling asleep at night? This phenomenon is not as unusual as it may seem.

Creative ideas are typically generated when the brain is in a relaxed state. The key to capturing the ideas before they evaporate is to have a pad and pen with you at all times. I keep a pad, pen, and small flashlight in my night table so I am prepared at those inopportune moments to capture creative thought.

THE MAP® SYSTEM OF GOAL SETTING

Another method of regaining perspective and control when you find that you're attempting to do too much is the "MAP"® system of goal setting.

The MAP system stands for *Minimum, Advanced, and Premium* goals. Think in terms of the number of calls you need to make each day. What is the *minimum* amount you can make and still leave feeling satisfied? Now suppose that your day is going smoothly; you have fewer interruptions than usual. What is an *advanced* number of calls that you can make? Now think of a perfect day—one where you can really stay on the phone and go for it. What would your *premium* number of calls be? The MAP system helps you set target call numbers to shoot for each day. Instead of having one goal (all or nothing), you have the choice of three. (See Table 3.12.) That way you have a greater probability for success.

Using MAP to Prioritize

The MAP system of goal setting can also be used in organizing the priority of your to-do list.

Many sales professionals learn to prioritize their to-do lists with priority letters, such as "A," "B," and "C" priorities. But what often happens is that soon everything becomes an A priority, and the A becomes an A++, or A+++, or A–. The differentiation of the importance and urgency of each priority becomes unclear.

By using the MAP, sales professionals make a commitment to accomplish their minimum goal on their to-do lists before they leave for the day. And then, if their day is less hectic than usual, they can strive to reach their advanced and premium goals, too. Having a three-tier goal gives your daily plan more flexibility while at the same time enabling you to keep track of what must get done.

Some salespeople create one MAP plan to conquer before lunch, and another to complete before the end of the day.

Since the typical to-do list has 24 to 36 items on it, and it would take approximately two to three days to accomplish everything on that list, it helps

TABLE 3.12 MAP YOUR CALLS AND TRACK RESULTS

Using the MAP system below as an example, keep track of the number of cold calls that you make during a specific time period (phone zone) and the results that you achieved, to determine whether you have reached or exceeded you goals.

| MAP System | Time frame: 2-hour phone zone | | |
	Dials	Connects	Appointments
Minimum	20	5	2
Advance	30	10	3
Premium	40	15	5

to have a system that cuts through to the critical tasks first.

Sales professionals who use the MAP system of goal setting:

- Accomplish more tasks
- Stay more focused on their goals
- Are more self-managed
- Feel less overwhelmed and anxious
- Waste less time
- Have more productive days
- Feel more motivated
- Leave work (the office) feeling more satisfied
- Make more sales!

BOTTOM **Without a MAP You Get Lost**
LINE With a MAP you know where you're going. Without one you get lost.

Phone Zones®

CONCEPT Another way for sales representatives to keep on track is through the development and implementation of phone zones.® A phone zone entails reserving or scheduling a block of time solely dedicated to making outbound sales phone calls. It is best to block this time in chunks on a calendar to keep committed to doing it. A phone zone can be just about any length of time—from six minutes to six hours. But, the ideal time frame for a phone zone is one to three hours. This substantial chunk of time enables momentum to build up. Table 3.12 shows a MAP for a two-hour phone zone.

Give the phone zone a try. Top sales producers report that the phone zone cumulatively over time leads to a significant increase in sales. It is one of the "best uses of their time and energy."

TIME ROBBER #5:
CONCEPT **INEFFECTIVE DELEGATION**

Many sales professionals have a difficult time delegating tasks, or responsibilities for the following reasons:

1. "No one to delegate to."
2. "I can do it faster myself."

3. "I can do it better myself."

4. "Only I have the ability to do it."

5. "I have no time to train the delegatee."

Have you found yourself using these excuses for not delegating? The reality is that delegating is beneficial to you, to your clients, and to your parent company. Once you learn specific steps to effective delegation, you will be delighted to discover how much time you can save. Many who resist delegation do so because they don't know how to. The old adage rings true: *"Never put off until tomorrow what you could have someone else do today."* (See Table 3.13.)

SIX STEPS TO INCREASE YOUR DELEGATION EFFECTIVENESS

Step 1: Pass It On

The first step to becoming an effective delegator is to look at all of your responsibilities, tasks, and day-to-day activities and ask yourself, "Why am I doing this?" "Who else could do it?" If the activity you are doing is time-consuming, routine, or you are no longer learning by performing the activity, you may need to "fire yourself" and pass it on. (See Table 3.14.)

Step 2: Delegate Up

Have you ever tried to get something accomplished either within your organization or with a client, and spent a lot of time getting nowhere? Then you see your boss about the matter—and he or she makes one phone call, and it's done!

Identify items on your to-do list that might advance faster—and achieve better results—by delegating them *up*.

TABLE 3.13 WHY DELEGATE?

- Allows for foresight
- Frees up time for client focus
- Enhances leadership skills
- Builds trust
- Increases productivity
- Increases profitability

TABLE 3.14 THE FOUR DIRECTIONS OF DELEGATION

1. Up—to your boss
2. Down—to your assistant
3. Sideways—to your peers
4. Out—to a temp, intern, or part-time helper

Step 3: Delegate Down

Delegating down is different than dumping. Unfortunately, most sales professionals approach it in a manner like this: "Hey you, come here. Please do this, thanks, see ya later." This is not effective delegation. It is dumping. The steps to effective delegation are detailed in the delegator's checklist in Table 3.15.

Step 4: Manage the Delegatee

Once you communicate your objectives clearly to the delegatee, get his or her input. By asking the right questions, you'll save time and get the results you want. Here are some sample questions that you might ask your delegatee:

- Please summarize/paraphrase what it is I need you to do.

- How will you go about doing this?

- What can I do to help you get started?

- When can you give me feedback on how it's going?

- Do you think that you can finish this on or ahead of the deadline? What might prevent you from reaching this goal on time?

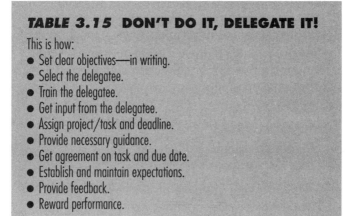

TABLE 3.15 DON'T DO IT, DELEGATE IT!

This is how:
- Set clear objectives—in writing.
- Select the delegatee.
- Train the delegatee.
- Get input from the delegatee.
- Assign project/task and deadline.
- Provide necessary guidance.
- Get agreement on task and due date.
- Establish and maintain expectations.
- Provide feedback.
- Reward performance.

- If you should find at any time that you might not meet the deadline, let me know at once.

Step 5: Delegate Sideways

Are there certain activities that you enjoy doing that your peers don't? What about vice versa? Delegating sideways is when you trade an activity that you don't like for one that your peer does like. By doing activities that you enjoy and are good at, you get through your responsibilities more quickly and with less effort. Reciprocation is the key.

Step 6: Delegate Out

When you have work to get done, and it is not the type of work you consider to be the best use of your time, you may need to utilize outside help to get the job done. Some examples of resources you could turn to are:

- Temporary employment services
- Interns
- High school students

BOTTOM LINE **FIRE YOURSELF!**

Fire yourself from tasks that take you away from generating sales revenue.

 **TIME ROBBER #6:**
CONCEPT **PROCRASTINATION**

Putting things off is a chronic time management problem. We naturally tend to migrate toward the quick and easy tasks, and leave the hard stuff for later . . . and later . . . and later. To-do items that take longer than 2 to 20 minutes get pushed aside. We tell ourselves that we'll do them when we can find an hour or two of uninterrupted time. Whenever that is! (Usually it is never.)

We're behind you all the way!
  Procrastination club credo

The following four-step process—*look, divide, begin,* and *reward*—can help you to conquer procrastination. By following each step, your work will get done sooner instead of later.

HOW TO STOP "PUTTING IT OFF"

To stop procrastinating and get more done, do this:

1. *Look* at the scope of what needs to be done.
2. *Divide* it into doable (preferably portable) chunks of 2 to 20 minutes each.
3. *Begin* by doing the first chunk.
4. *Reward* yourself for the accomplishment.

Step 1: Look at the Scope

Look at the total picture of what needs to be done. Determine all the necessary action steps. Estimate how long the entire task will take to complete.

Step 2: Divide

A doable chunk is approximately 2 to 20 minutes of work. It is a manageable chunk of time within which you can actually get something done. Breaking the project down stops you from trying to do too much at once and getting frustrated. In essence, "don't try to boil the ocean." Instead, take consistent "baby steps" that will yield big results over time.

Also, make sure that your doable chunks are portable. Do you find that there are times in your day when you need to wait for things? According to *Ripley's Believe It or Not,* we spend six years of our lives "waiting," for meetings, in line, at doctors' and dentists' offices.

If you bring your doable chunks with you (in a briefcase, tote, clipboard or file folder) and work on them during unexpected waiting times you will find that you can successfully chip away at your workload and get more done in less time.

Step 3: Begin the First Task

Begin at the beginning. There is a lot of truth to the old adage that "a job begun is a job half-done." Once you finish the first doable chunk, you'll be on to the next—and so on, and so on, straight through to completion.

Step 4: Reward Yourself

Behavior that gets rewarded is usually repeated. (So say psychology studies on motivation.) Without rewards, there is little incentive to focus on breaking goals down and conquering procrastination. Ways of rewarding yourself include:

- Take a short break
- Self-praise—All right!
- M&M's. (Yum!)
- Call a friend
- Touch base with a friendly client
- Two pats on the back (and a rub)
- Stretch and relax

BOTTOM LINE JUST DO IT!

"Just Do It!" Divide and conquer. Or, as Mother Teresa once said, *"You can do no great things in life, only little things with great love."*

TIME MANAGEMENT EQUALS SELF MANAGEMENT

Time management is really self management. By applying the time management and self-management key concepts and tips listed in this chapter, you will gain hundreds of minutes per week. Achieving success in controlling your time takes awareness, discipline, and practice. But the results are well worth the effort because you will feel less stress and increase sales activity and revenue. This will in turn positively influence your sales success rate.

Getting and Staying Connected

Some succeed because they are destined to, most succeed because they are determined to.

Anatole France

Self-managed selling takes discipline. One form of discipline is getting and staying connected with prospects and clients. For some, the word "discipline" might suggest a harsh or even painful process. Yet, it may be beneficial to reflect on which pain is greater—the pain of discipline, or the pain of regret.

After many years of serving as a consultant to sales professionals, I am hard-pressed to come up with any top-flight, self-managed sales professional who has regretted taking the time doing what was necessary to become highly self-disciplined. The risks these sales professionals take for the sake of personal growth and profit, as well as creative client problem-solving, are well worth it.

The trouble is, if you don't risk anything, you risk even more.

Erica Jong

By following the specific "how-to" guidelines in this chapter, you will discover how to get and stay connected with your customers by:

- Targeting your market
- Approaching new clients
- Building business partnerships and alliances
- Selling at higher levels

- Staying Visible: Being at the forefront of your customer's mind

Self-managed, well disciplined behavior starts with understanding and embracing the "connection process."

THE CONNECTION PROCESS

Sales is a contact sport. The more targeted "connects" you make, the higher the probability of your success. The connection process involves making essential decisions regarding who to connect with. Often, in sales, there is a vast array of people you can sell your product or service to. For some products and services, almost anyone might be a potential customer. While this can be both exhilarating and overwhelming, in most cases, managing your sales effort independently means aiming at a well-defined, specific market.

The primary types of sales connections, and their corresponding business potential are as follows:

- *Suspect Connection:* A vendor that you think or suspect may want to do business with you. Business potential: Unknown, but hopeful.

- *Prospect Connection:* A vendor where there is a strong likelihood that what you are selling is what the customer needs, wants, and can afford to buy. Business potential: Very good.

- *Past (Dormant) Customer Connection:* A customer who has once bought from you, or your organization, but no longer does. Business potential: Rejuvenation is often possible, and at times highly probable, depending on the former customer's reasons for leaving.

- *Existing Customer Connection:* A customer with whom you are currently doing business. Business potential: The best business potential for linking and leveraging new business while maintaining the current relationship.

- *Competitor's Customer Connection:* The customer of a competitor. Business potential: Very good. If they have the money and are buying the product, one false move by your rival (i.e., poor quality, delayed delivery, etc.), and you may well be in.

- *Referral Connection:* Someone who refers business to you. Business potential: Excellent! Personal introductions and name-dropping yield a high probability of success.

- *Trade Show/Business Event Connection:* A person you meet at a trade show or business event. Business potential: Excellent! (I personally can't recall attending any trade show or business event that I didn't make money from!)

Regardless of whether you are connecting with a suspect, prospect, past (dormant) customer, existing customer, a competitor's customer, or referral or trade show lead, you are just a "call" away from determining if you are moving closer to or further away from winning a sale.

Let's explore each "connection" category and gain some insight into how to best utilize them.

Suspects/Prospects

Suspects/prospects are usually found in directories. A few examples would be *Standard and Poor's Register of Corporations, Directors, and Executives;* Dun & Bradstreet (D&B) Million Dollar Database, *The Million Dollar Directory; MacRay's* State Industrial Directory *Blue Book;* the Yellow Pages; and your local business-to-business or chamber of commerce directory and SIC Code Directory, to name a few. Industry trade association membership lists can also be a useful source to gather your leads. Use the qualifying questions later in this chapter to determine which suspects could turn into prospects.

Past (Dormant) Customers

These customers are usually found in a database, filing cabinet, and through old accounts receivable. Since business circumstances and personnel are in a constant state of flux, rekindling a dormant customer relationship is essential strategy to selling.

Recognize Your Fear, and Call Anyway

Be alert to any apprehension you might have toward calling a past account. Sometimes "scary" notes from a previous sales rep in the database, or a bad experience you had years ago with an account will make you reluctant to reconnect.

...portant to remember that in sales at any ...ou can get any reaction, from anyone ...pick up that phone, dial that number, ...be ready for anything!

Existing Customers

An existing customer is a key place to focus your time and attention. It is 80 percent easier to nurture existing business than it is to seek out new business. At the same time, however, it's easy to get complacent with existing business. It is critical to keep thinking of ways to expand existing business by seeking out new opportunities in different divisions, branches, or affiliations of current clients. Take a close look at what you have in your business relationship and then take a minute to brainstorm many of the possibilities that "might be." Make sure you are really getting the most potential business out of each of your client relationships. Why settle for *less* when *more* is possible?

Keep Filling the Sales Funnel

One downside to focusing too keenly on servicing your existing accounts is that along the course of business you may lose one or two (many times for reasons you can't control), and if you do, you might be headed toward trouble without having back-up prospects in your arsenal. It is always best to carefully nurture and leverage existing business as you simultaneously and continuously set new and expanded sales goals. That way you can generate more business with minimal risk and still be covered.

Competitor's Customers

It is easier in some industries to discover which companies are working with your competition than it is in others. In advertising sales it's impossible to hide. There it is, printed in the glossy color pages of your biggest competitor's book (magazine). (And the prospect's ad agency said that the client had no budget!?)

One way to find out who a suspect/prospect is working with is to ask. What's the worst thing that can happen? They might tell you, "It's none of your business." But hey, if you're in sales and have never been told that before, you haven't been asking enough of the right probing questions.

To smoke out the competition in a less crude, more sophisticated way, you might finesse your questioning with a touch of politeness by asking, "Would you mind my asking whether you are considering working with any other product or service?" This bit of disarming linguistic gymnastics allows you to ask but gives the illusion that you haven't breached any barriers. Before you know it, you can learn vital information regarding any competitor.

Referrals

Referrals unlock the bolted doors in business better than just about any other source. If you are fortunate, your clients, friends, and family members will provide you with unsolicited referrals. But of course one of the most effective ways to get referrals is to ask for them!

How and When to Ask for Referrals

The best time to ask for a referral is immediately after you have received a compliment or made a sale. If you plan ahead on asking for referrals as soon as you see the opportune moment, you will achieve the best results. So, how do you ask? What exactly do you say? Many sales professionals, when asking for referrals, will say, "Do you happen to know anyone who you feel might also benefit from using my product or service? Usually the reply is, "Hmmm," or possibly "Let me think about that and get back to you." (And they don't.)

To get the best results, ask specific questions, rather than the vague "Who do you know?" Specific questions yield specific responses. For example, ask, "What other division in your company could also benefit from using our products or services?" Or, "Who do you know who has a similar position to yours—perhaps a vice president of marketing in a different company—who might be able to benefit from my products or services?"

A third way to make a specific referral request is to ask, "Could you please tell me an association that you belong to that may have members who could also benefit from my product or service?" Once the client/prospect gives you the name of the referral, it is essential to immediately follow up with this line of questioning: "Would you mind my asking the name of the best contact?" "Do you know his or her title?" "Do you happen to have a phone number, possibly a direct dial?" "May I use your name when I call?"

Finally, on every referral received, remember to thank the person who made the referral and keep him or her in the loop regarding the outcome.

Trade Shows/Business Events

This connection category is typically referred to as *event-driven marketing.* In essence, it involves getting a whole bunch of business professionals together, and seeing how much revenue they can generate through alliances they can form by meeting one another.

How do you "work" a trade show or business event? Do you stay with your colleagues and wait for people to come over and introduce themselves to you? Or, do you set a goal for the number of contacts you seek to meet and go after them? See Table 4.1 for additional information on how to get the best results from attending a trade show.

Be a "Star"

The expression "Maintain the campaign" comes to mind when I think about seeking business opportunities at trades show or business events. I first became aware of this concept when reading a book entitled *Rogers' Rules For Success* by Henry

---

TABLE 4.1 HOW TO "WORK" A TRADE SHOW/BUSINESS EVENT

- Set a goal: Decide on the approximate number of contacts you want to make.
- Strive to reach your goal: Break out of your comfort zone. Seek out speaking opportunities with people who can provide business opportunities for you.
- Wear a suit with two pockets: Use the left pocket for your cards and the right one for theirs.
- Wear a color of suit or tie that is memorable, to stand out from the rest.
- Write on the back of each business card you collect the date, the event, and the purpose of the follow-up.
- Follow-up on each lead within 24 to 36 hours of the event.

C. Rogers, of Rogers and Cohen Public Relations. In his book, Rogers says that when you are out and meeting people it is important to act as though you are running for political office. Exude an aura of confidence; be friendly and personable; have a positive spirit and outlook. Event-driven marketing provides you with some of the best-available business exposure and visibility. Use this opportunity to your biggest advantage. You will greatly benefit if you think of these events as "your time to shine!"

Once you have gathered your target marketing connections and sources, the next step is qualifying those sources. A good way to qualify those that fall within your potential target market is through asking a series of qualifying questions.

SALES IS A CONTACT SPORT: PRIMARY TYPES OF EFFECTIVE SALES CONNECTIONS

Suspect: A company that you think may want to do business with you.

   Business potential: Unknown, but hopeful.

Prospect: A strong likelihood you'll do business together.

   Business potential: Very good.

Past (Dormant) Customer Connections: A previous customer.

   Business potential: Rejuvenation is very likely.

Existing Customer Connections: A customer who you are doing business with now.

   Business potential: The best business potential for linking and leveraging new business while maintaining the current relationship.

Competitor's Customer: A customer of a competitor.

   Business potential: Very good. One false move or reorganization and you may very well "be in."

Referrals: A person who refers business to you.

   Business potential: Excellent. A high success probability.

Trade Shows: A person you meet at a trade show.

   Business potential: Excellent. Tremendous visibility.

TARGET YOUR CONNECTIONS BY ASKING QUALIFYING QUESTIONS

Asking yourself qualifying questions while targeting your market is a tremendous time-saver. Here are a few strategic qualifying questions to ask:

• Do they need my product/service?

- What unique, creative, "customer-focused" business solutions can I provide?
- What improvements will this suspect/prospect gain by working with me?
- Can they afford buying my product/service?
- Who else might be providing this suspect/prospect a similar service to mine?
- What advantages does my company have over the competition, our "edge"?
- What would it take to make a suspect/prospect switch from a competitor to me?
- Is this the right sized company for me to approach?
- What leveraging opportunities exist within this organization that I am targeting?
- On a scale of 1 to 10, with 10 being the highest, what is the likelihood of this person or company becoming my customer? (If the answer is not within the 8 to 10 range, what would be required to move it up to an 8 to 10?)
- Does this suspect/prospect seem worthwhile?
- What does my "gut" say about pursuing this account?
- What's the worst thing that could happen?
- What's the best thing that could happen?

MAKE THAT CALL

Sales is not an exact science—it's a "probable occurrence." Therefore, a good rule of thumb when analyzing your marketing calls is, "When in doubt, don't rule it out." You never know. But, be careful about targeting too many long shots. Calculated, educated risks yield more viable results than random (reckless) risk-taking.

DEVELOP A CALLER LIST

When making calls in the pursuit of new business, it is best to develop a "call list." It makes little difference whether your call list is computer generated, or handwritten; having a list with all of your calls for the day/week will enhance your call-to-connection ratio. A call list simply entails having the name, title, company name, phone number, fax number, and purpose of your call all in one place. When you have to look up numbers and figure out the purpose of each call as you go, the process becomes disorganized, erratic, and frustrating.

Ideally, your call list should be portable so that nothing can prevent you from making that next call. Whether you are at the office, in a taxi, driving your car, or at the airport pay phone, having your call list readily available at all times will drastically impact your annual revenue stream. (See Table 4.2.)

BOTTOM LINE — MORE CALLS EQUALS MORE SALES

Target your market, then make your calls. The more calls, the more connects; the more connects, the more appointments; the more appointments, the more sales; the more sales, the more commission. Everybody wins! When you analyze it, it really is as simple as that.

KEY CONCEPT — SELL AT HIGHER LEVELS

The concept of selling at higher levels is also referred to as _top-down selling._ Starting at the top means calling the highest levels of the organization chart, and then working your way down to the appropriate decision maker. There are many benefits to top-down selling, including these:

● There are more decision makers at the top.

● When you start at the top and are referred down, your call has a better chance of being responded to than if you call cold.

TABLE 4.2 CALLS THAT INCREASE PRODUCTIVITY

CALL LIST

Name	Company Title	Phone name	Purpose number	of the call
1. Bill Gordon	CFO	Charlington Corp.	222.555.1234	Seek a company visit
2. Jane Yar	V.P., H.R.	Crane Inc.	331.555.0988	Qualify & meet
3. John Williams	Purchasing	DBO Int'l	456.555.9800	Referred by Joe Gore
4. Carla Jones	COO	Harris & Lundberg	556.555.8787	Association networking

- You can reconnect with the top without feeling like you're going over anyone's head, because that's where you started.

When Calling "the Top" Be Clear and Concise

When selling at the top, you need to understand the culture. There is usually less time for idle chitchat and rapport building, and more need for crystallizing your specific purpose for the call—the clear, compelling "dollars-and-sense" reasons for them to meet with you, and the beneficial results you intend to provide. As a general rule, people at the top live in a world that is concise, to the point, and results-oriented (with "results" more often than not meaning "revenue").

Perseverance is the great element of success. If you just knock long enough and loud enough at the gate, you are sure to wake somebody up.

Longfellow

The Gatekeeper Factor

On your enthusiastic beeline to the top, there may be a few hurdles to fly over along the way. The classic term is *gatekeeper*—however, if you think of gatekeepers as obstacles you'll have a harder time reaching your destination. It has been said that "obstacles" are only those things you see when you have lost sight of your goal. I like to think of the gatekeepers as allies who assist rather than prevent me from getting where I need to go.

Twelve Ways to Get to the Top, over the Hurdles and through the Gates

- Use the phrase, "I need your help."
- Ask Reception for the direct-line number.
- Call after-hours and use the automated directory to get the direct dial.
- Search the company's Internet/Web page for the best contact information.
- Send an e-mail. Ask for/guess the address.
- Call Accounts Payable. This is an old recruiting trick. Say you're lost in the system and tell them who you're looking for, and ask for direct dial.

They may be so relieved that you're not angry about an unpaid bill that they'll put you right through.

- Befriend the secretary/receptionist.
- Ask the gatekeeper how to spell his or her name. If you ask a person named Michelle if it's one l or two you will gain a friend for life.
- Ask, "Do you keep his/her calendar?" Book an appointment.
- Call early; or late; or during lunch. I've had very good luck connecting with top-level decision makers at 7:00 A.M. and 7:00 P.M.

CALL EARLY + LATE

- If you keep getting voice mail, press 0. Ask the person who answers if the person you are calling ever picks up his or her extension, and when the best time is to reach him or her.
- Use the "Call 'til you get him or her" approach. But leaving more than one or two messages can seem pushy—so, if you know the contact answers his or her own phone, call until you connect, without leaving several messages. (In case the prospect has Caller ID, use this technique, but call through reception, or block your ID so as to avoid being viewed as a stalker.)

call through reception to avoid callerid

DANGER! **Don't Make Assumptions**

You never know who the gatekeeper might be. In smaller companies he or she could be someone closely related to the decision maker. Therefore, never assume your comments are safe with this person. Most gatekeepers are very influential and can often determine whether you'll get in.

The "I Just Need to Know" Technique

Many times when you finally do get to the decision-maker, after spending great time and effort navigating the sale (and at times sailing through rough and choppy waters to get there), the person you reach is too busy to speak. The response may be, "I'm in a meeting," or "I can't speak to you right now," and you may rush off the phone with a quick, "Okay, bye."

Instead, acknowledge their response and go a little further by saying, "It sounds like you're very busy. I just needed to know if you're free Tuesday at 2:00 P.M. to meet." Or "I just need to know if you use vacuum-powered air filters at your plant." Or "I just needed to know when a better time to call you would be."

When you wind up a rushed conversation with the disarming phrase I just need to know, and make your question very direct (closed-ended) you will get more information to further the sale.

If you don't prepare the "I just needed to know" question, you will use "Okay, bye," which gets you nowhere in the process.

Overcoming the Fear Factor

A good deal of fear and self-doubt occurs when going through the process of top-down selling. Thoughts of uncertainty seep in—crazy thoughts like, "I'm not worthy to talk to anyone at this level." Or, "He/she will be too busy to speak to me." Or, call-reluctance/avoidance thoughts like, "Now's probably not a good time to call." My response to that particular comment is that anytime is a good time if you have something of value to offer.

And yes, you are worthy, if you can provide creative business solutions that will directly and positively impact revenue.

As long as you strongly believe in yourself and your product or service, you earn the right to make the call.

KEY CONCEPT   GETTING IN THE DOOR: SAYING THE RIGHT THING

When approaching new top-level prospects or existing/dormant clients, what you say and how you say it will be critical to your success. Once you have formed an alliance with your gatekeeper and get the direct dial, or are transferred through, you need to be fully prepared regarding what to say and how to say it.

I remember once years ago, being so intent on connecting with a referral that I called relentlessly. I was determined to get hold of him. His secretary Maria helped me to zero in. She said he was a morning person and that he did answer his own phone. That's all I needed to know. I decided that I was going to call him very early the next morning at 15-minute intervals until I got him.

So the next day I awoke at 6:00 A.M., and at 6:30 I dialed the number; there was no answer. At

6:45, still no answer; at 7:00 I heard him say, "Darren Zonsky," at which time I said, "Oh my god!" and hung up.

I had become so focused on getting Darren that I hadn't given much thought to what to say when I got him. Of course I did call him back 30 minutes later (thank goodness this occurred before the advent of Caller ID), at which time I finally was fully prepared, stated my purpose for calling, and eventually got the business.

Connecting on the Phone: Voice-to-Voice

So what *do* you say when, after weeks of follow-up, you actually get that person? Here are a few suggestions:

When connecting voice-to-voice, first introduce yourself and your company and explain the purpose of your call. Then ask a brief involvement question. Example: "Good morning Joe, this is Joy Baldridge, from Baldridge Seminars International. The purpose of my call is to share new ideas with you regarding sales training. How do you currently train your sales force?" (Open-ended question.) Or, "Do you provide sales training for your reps?" (Closed-ended.) "When can we meet to discuss this further?" (Closed-ended.)

Always remember your ABCs when making connection calls. "ABC" stands for *Always Be Closing.* Once you've established who you are, where you're from, the purpose of your call, and have asked your involvement question, you need to "close." The close can be seeking an appointment by asking, "When can we meet?" Or, it can be setting up a follow-up phone conversation for the next week. You can even close by getting referred to the right person in the process. A close is nothing more than taking the process to the next step, with the ultimate step being to get a positive decision.

When calling a prospect/client, generally avoid asking "Do you have a minute?" or, "Is this a bad time?" Such a question gives the person you're calling a quick way to end the conversation. Some sales professionals say that they never ask these types of questions because of that reason. But many others say they do as a courtesy. So what's the best approach? To go with your gut. If the person you are calling sounds harried, that is a good time to ask. But instead of saying, "Is this a bad time?" it is better to say, "Is this a good time?" The reason is twofold: (1) The person you're calling is more likely to say yes than no; and (2) It's a polite gesture that shows that you respect the person's time schedule.

CALL BACK ON A GOOD DAY

When my friend Julie was making a connection call, she used the "Is this a good time?" phrase, as she felt the contact person sounded rushed. The contact quickly responded with an emphatic "No!" Then Julie politely asked, "When would be a good time?" "Maybe a year or two from now," was the gruff reply. Being a professional, Julie did not go on to ask if she should call in the morning or afternoon a year or two from now. She simply said, "It sounds like you're incredibly busy. I'll just give you a call later on to touch base."

Julie immediately scheduled a note in her Act database to call back three months later. When she did, she was very well received. The contact was so open and friendly that Julie felt compelled to say, "Do you remember what you said the last time I called you?" To Julie's surprise, the woman had completely forgotten her tense rejection! When Julie reminded her that "You told me to call in a year or two," the contact seemed stunned, apologized, and offered to meet right away.

Don't be rattled or intimidated by a customer's crazy day. Many salespeople feel like they are a bother or an intrusion; squash those negative thoughts. Don't flee when you meet adversity. A second call at a later time can turn out to be very productive.

Thoughts are very powerful creatures. Always remember, what "they" think means nothing, what "you" think means everything!

(unknown author)

Connecting on Voice Mail

There is a certain etiquette regarding voice mail that when used will result in more return phone calls. Try this:

- Say "Good morning" or "Good afternoon," which sounds more professional than "Hi!"
- Introduce your company.

- State your phone number clearly and slowly. (Speak at the rate people write.)
- State the purpose of your call.
- Say your name and phone number again clearly and enthusiastically.
- Say, "The best time of day to reach me: (between 10:00 a.m. and noon.)"
- Close with a phrase like, "I look forward to your return call."

When leaving a voice mail message it's essential that you project a positive, upbeat voice tone, mood, and manner. You need to sound like someone the listener will want to talk to and work with, and call back.

Intention

The salespeople I have surveyed who receive the most return phone calls are those who make calls with "intention." They report that when they leave a message on voice mail, they make a point to have their voice convey an expectation that the call will be returned. Having the tone of intention in your voice, and doing it in a friendly manner will get you more return calls. Try it and see!

LEARNED HELPLESSNESS

When you start making your calls and you hit a lot of dead ends (i.e., people saying no; or being too busy to talk to you; or rude gatekeepers and endless voice mail), you can start to feel like you're not getting anywhere. Repeated rejection can start to rob your spirit, lower your self-esteem, and destroy your enthusiasm. You can actually *learn* to be helpless, which means that when you finally do get to that call that will open up doors, your helplessness may hinder your chances of success.

An illustration: Some psychologists experimented with fleas that were capable of jumping three times higher than the top of a particular jar. They put the fleas in the jar and put a lid on the jar. The fleas would jump and hit the lid, jump and hit the lid. When the lid was finally removed, despite the fact that the fleas had the capacity to jump three times the height of the jar, how high do you think they jumped? They jumped to the height of the jar and no higher. Have you ever experienced learned helplessness? You make call after call and get nowhere and then finally, when an opportunity is found, for which you need to jump beyond the height of the jar, you become an unwilling victim of learned helplessness.

One sales professional said she called 20 people about a product demonstration she wanted to set up with them. Of course she started her first call with great energy and enthusiasm, but by the 20th call her voice mail messages were sounding canned, burned out, and hurried. When she finally did get someone on the phone that actually wanted to see her demonstration, she slipped and replied incredulously, "You do?!" Fortunately, she experienced a huge adrenaline rush, recovered quickly, and set it up.

It is important to remember that learned help-lessness is real. And it can seep into your soul and start creating a negative mind-set.

Fall down seven times, stand up eight.
Japanese proverb

Practice/Rehearse

In sales as in most other things, you can't under-estimate the importance of practice. Many sales professionals do not like scripts, because they think that they will sound canned, rehearsed, and unnatural. Many just "wing it" and hope for the best. But, there is a way to have a script and sound natural. You can practice on the phone or by writing your script on paper.

On the phone: Call your own voice mail and leave your rehearsed message. Then listen to it and ask yourself, "Would you call you back?" Or you can recite it to yourself until it feels right.

On the page: Script out what you plan to say, using emphasis marks to convey the appropriate tone. For example, use an *up tone, down tone,* or *pause.* Circle any word you want to punch with enthusiasm. Put two vertical lines between words for pauses for impact, and put ascending arrows (↑) above words that you want to end on an upbeat tone and descending arrows (↓) above those you want to end on a serious tone.

Example: "Good morning! This is Joy Baldridge, from Baldridge Seminars International at (phone number). The purpose of my call is to discuss revenue-driven sales training ideas for your sales representatives. Again, this is Joy Baldridge, at (phone number). I look forward to your return call."

Model: Good morning! This is _____ from _____ at (____) _____. The purpose of my call is _____. Again this is _____ at (____) _____. I look forward to your return call.

In the preceding model, fill in the information that you would say when leaving your voice mail message. Once you have filled in all of your information, read it aloud in a natural way and write in your emphasis marks whenever they seem appropriate.

Keep It Short

Time yourself. Look at the second hand of your watch for a starting time. Read your voice mail message with genuine feeling, using the emphasis marks for proper pausing and voice inflection, then look at your time when you've finished reading. Ideally, introductory voice mail messages should be 18 to 22 seconds in length, without sounding rushed or rehearsed.

The Human Touch

Somewhere in your message it is critical to add a human touch. One way is to use their name. Sound sincere.

Use your voice tone to indicate that you are a real person or give the person you are calling a real (good) reason to call you back. For instance: The purpose of my call is to show you a more efficient way to run accounting reports. I'm sure a lot of people call you about this matter, but if you want to save time and be efficient, I'm the one you need to call.

To be nobody but yourself in a world which is doing its best, day and night to make you like everybody else, is to fight the hardest battle any human can fight—but never stop fighting.

e. e. cummings

Take a Risk

Once in a while taking a risk when leaving a voice mail message pays off. One salesperson, Vicki,

THE CONNECTION PROCESS:
WHAT TO SAY

Voice-to-Voice Guidelines

1. Introduce yourself.
2. Introduce your company.
3. State the purpose of your call.
4. Ask an involvement question.
5. Close for an appointment.
6. Voice tone, mood and manner must be friendly, upbeat, enthusiastic and positive.

Voice-to-Voice Mail Guidelines

1. Say "Good morning" or "Good afternoon."
2. Introduce yourself.
3. Introduce your company.
4. Clearly and slowly state your phone number
5. State the purpose of your call.
6. Say your name and phone number again, slowly, clearly, and enthusiastically.
7. Close with a phrase like, "I look forward to your return call."

when she feels she's not getting enough return calls tries her Wonder Woman routine. On her third or fourth attempt to reach the contact person she'll say, "This is so and so from XYZ Company, also known as Wonder Woman. I can fight crime and scale high walls, but I can't seem to get you to return my call." As hokey as it sounds, she gets return calls this way. The key is to do something different from the rest of the pack. But make sure you feel good about your "out-of-the-box" stunt, and management approves of it.

Another approach that Vicki takes to getting more return phone calls from voice mails she has left is as follows:

"I say, you must be like the Loch Ness monster, because legend has it that you both exist, but I haven't seen or heard from you, so give me a call to prove you exist." Hey, it works for her!

Another person, Julie, who works with Vicki, tried this approach:

"Hi, this is Julie from X Corp. Are you the invisible man? Because you are impossible to find. Materialize by calling me at _____."

Julie did get a return call, but it was a week after leaving the message. She had forgotten all about it. The caller said, "Hi Julie, this is Joel Weis. I am returning your call to tell you I am not invisible."

Julie was so flabbergasted all she could think to say was, "That's nice." Then she quickly collected her thoughts and went after an appointment.

"Why not?" is a slogan for an interesting life.
Mason Cooley

BOTTOM **Increase Your Success**

LINE Preparing for both voice-to-voice or voice mail increases your probability for success. On the whole, people like to do business with people who (1) speak with enthusiasm and intention; (2) communicate clearly; (3) seem to have a specific purpose driving them; (4) are seeking action; and (5) convey a human/humorous element. These are all characteristics of successful self-managed sales professionals.

 STAY VISIBLE

CONCEPT Getting and staying connected has everything to do with staying visible. Having many points of contact increases your probability for staying at the forefront of your prospect/customer's mind. (See Table 4.3.)

There are an infinite number of ways to get and stay visible. In the following pages you will find a detailed summary of the 12 Viable Visibility

---

TABLE 4.3 TWELVE VIABLE VISIBILITY VENUES

Send, Send, Send:

- Postcards
- A-OKs. Always Offer [thoughtful and well-researched] Knowledge
- Personal note cards
- Faxes
- E-mails
- Cartoons
- Promotion premiums
- Announcements
- Outrageous stuff

Go, Go, Go to:

- Association events
- Trade seminars
- Networking functions

Venues shown in Table 4.3. They are all part of "maintaining the campaign."

Visibility Venue #1: Send Postcards

Postcards are a quick, inexpensive, and tangible way to stay visible. They are also "clutter-busters." When people peruse their mail, a postcard will definitely and quickly not only rise to the top, but it will also get read. Plus, they are fun and easy to write, so you can get 8 to 10 done and mailed in the time it would take to do 1 or 2 follow-up letters.

It seems there are postcards of everything these days. I sent a postcard of a cup of cappuccino to a prospect and the reverse side said, "Time for a break, let's meet for coffee."

When traveling, I'll send a card, say, from Los Angeles, to my New York prospects/clients saying: "Greetings from LA! I'm out here conducting some sales seminars. Give you a call when I return to discuss some new training ideas! All the best, Joy."

If you pick a postcard that is tastefully funny or has a stunningly beautiful scene, you will get ten times the exposure. The goal is to select a "bulletin-board-worthy"® postcard. I can't tell you how many times I have walked into offices of my prospects/clients and seen my postcard on their bulletin board. The result: visibility—another positive point of contact and rapport-strengthening penetration. Plus—everyone else sees the postcard and asks "Who's it from? Who is she? Trés cool!"

Take a Systematic Approach

For the best postcard results you should:

- Buy a roll of 100 self-adhesive postcard stamps to take with you.

- Print out your Rolodex and bring it with you. (or bring your palm pilot or laptop)

- As soon as you reach your destination, scout out the cards that you think will elicit a positive reaction.

- Always mail the postcards before leaving the city they are from. (Wouldn't *you* look to see whether it was mailed as a thoughtful gesture from the city itself, or as an afterthought once the sender got home?) Believe me, they *always* look at the postmark.

- Write a message that is simple—a few brief sentences basically conveying, "I am here, and this is what I'm doing for XYZ Co. I can also do it for you; let's connect when I return."

After you have sent a postcard, something almost always happens . . . a magical thing. When you make your follow-up phone call, instead of getting a chilly, resistant response, you get an enthusiastic "I got your postcard!" greeting, and it feels terrific! Try it and see!

Great R.O.I. (Return On Investment)

I'm hooked on the postcard visibility concept, mainly because I enjoy writing and sending post-cards—but also because I get results. I can directly link a quarter of a million dollars' worth of business within a two-year period that resulted from sending hundreds of 50-cent postcards with 20-cent stamps. Not a bad return on an investment!

My all-time best record of postcard sending was achieved on a trip to New Orleans. I wanted to send 175 postcards (since New Orleans is an exciting place and happens to have cool postcards). I was only going to be in town for two days and I knew I couldn't possibly get them all written, addressed, stamped, and mailed in 48 hours. So several weeks before the trip I called the Marriott, where I had a reservation, and was connected with the gift shop. I asked if I could charge 175 postcards on my Visa, and have them mailed to me; of course I would pay for the postage too. I gave the shop person a general idea of the purpose and the tone I wanted to set. (This avoided any French Quarter shocker cards.) The shop person agreed! I received the cards two weeks prior to my trip and diligently addressed them by hand. (To heighten the personal touch, I never use mailing labels.) I wrote each message, applied the self-adhesive stamps to all 175 postcards, packed them in my briefcase, and as soon as I deplaned I looked for a mailbox at the New Orleans airport—and they were on their way. The response was overwhelming! Tremendous! (And the advance preparation made the trip far less stressful.)

Visibility Venue #2: Send A-OKs

A-OK stands for "Always Offer Knowledge." Most people, including your prospects/clients, like to learn. If you see an appropriate article in the *Wall Street Journal* or *Fast Company* magazine, clip it, attach a note (e.g., "Thought this might interest you"), and send it off. The gesture is thoughtful and intelligent, and you are sharing knowledge for the sake of enlightenment or self-improvement. Most people make the decision to buy from you based on a desire to improve themselves, their staff, or their organization.

Check Your Sources

Although most people like to obtain useful knowledge from just about anywhere, be careful of the sources you choose. Your credibility will be connected to the reputation of the magazine, trade journal, or newspaper that you cite. So, choose your sources wisely.

Get Through to the Personal Side of Business

One way of selling A-OK's that goes beyond the norm of just sending business information is to break through to the personal side of business. One of my clients went on a sales call and during the course of the conversation discovered the contact person had a son who was an all-star lacrosse player. His son was scouting out colleges solely based on their lacrosse team's status. Finding a scholarship at a quality college with a stellar lacrosse team was no easy feat.

Upon returning to his office, my client got on the Internet and searched for all of the U.S. colleges with high-rated lacrosse teams. He assembled the information and sent it over with his proposal. It wasn't a bribe—simply a parent-to-parent courtesy. (He made the sale.)

Visibility Venue #3: Note Cards

With the tremendous influx of communication technology, the traditional handwritten note card is rapidly becoming more and more unique. Yet, it remains a great way to break through and stay visible.

Note card sending can be organized so that it becomes an effortless process. As long as you have all the tools, you'll find it an excellent way to keep in touch and not the chore you might expect it to be. I treat note card writing like a business. A file drawer containing my card supplier is right next to my desk. I have a pendoflex filled with interesting and unusual stamps, as well as pendoflexes full of cards in categories such as floral, aviation, wildlife, and nature. Also, a few general categories such as: birthday, anniversary, sympathy, serious, funny, inspirational, and so forth. While shopping, if you see cards that make you smile, laugh, or sigh, buy all of them. I guarantee they will be put to good use.

Aside from stationery shops, some of the most esthetic and relatively low-priced notepaper and note cards can be found in museum gift shops.

If you find a particularly good card, you may want to order a large quantity of them. If so, look on the back of the card for the manufacturer and call it directly. This way you can get a large supply for wholesale prices.

Also, be sure to document in your client database to whom you have sent which card, and indicate frequency and variety for further tracking your point of contact.

The Elements of Note Card Writing

The tools necessary for effective note card writing are:

- A good fine pen with crisp black or blue ink. (Do you have a preference? I only enjoy blue ink myself.)

- A variety of interesting-looking postage stamps to choose from—botanical garden flowers, fighter airplanes, and so forth.

- Rich-looking, top-quality note cards and notepaper, such as Crane's notepaper (Note: square note cards require additional postage regardless of size or weight.)

- A supply of gender-specific note cards.

- Your corporate note card.

- Legible, neat, and interesting handwriting. Spending a night or two in a school calligraphy course or practicing a little with a calligraphy book quickly yields some stylish messages.

- A scratch pad for scribbling out the first draft of your message content and layout—you'll save a fortune practicing on scrap paper before writing on the real thing. (After some practice, you can get your message right the first time if you start smaller and focus on staying horizontal.)

Visibility Venue #4: Faxes

Faxes can still act as clutter-busters despite the fact that they are so common. Eye-catching transmittals help. The beauty of a fax is that unlike a letter, it doesn't have to be opened. If you keep the information brief, it can quickly be glanced at and absorbed or dealt with.

I always like to send faxes along with a pertinent cartoon. I was once in the recruiting business. Like every other employment agency, I would send an abundance of resumes to clients. Later, I would call the client. Time after time when I asked, "Did you get my fax?" they would say "No." Then I had to refax and reconnect—a real waste of time.

Then, one day I saw a humorous cartoon pertaining to the interviewing process. I faxed it, along with three resumes. I called to ask if my client got my fax, and he said "No," once again! I said, "Are you sure? It was the one with the cartoon." He said, "Oh yeah, I got that one! It's right here."

Follow Up Fast

Quick follow-up is necessary when using faxing as a visibility tool. Faxes come fast—and they can also go fast.

Visibility Venue #5: E-Mail

Some love it and some loathe it, but regardless of how you feel about e-mail, it is here to stay. E-mail is a very direct way of being visible. It gets you right in. And the response effort is so simple. One client I spoke to said she never listens to her voice mail anymore, but is completely in tune and responsive to her e-mail. (She now delegates the voice mail to her assistant, who puts a summary of current voice mail messages in her e-mail.)

Turn to the Web

If you are having trouble getting an e-mail address that you need, try looking up the company's web site. Also, send attachments in color to further draw the recipient in.

Visibility Venue #6: Cartoons

The beauty of cartoons is that they put people into a positive mood. Carefully selected cartoons can lighten a day or elicit a laugh. When the person you're trying to connect with has that kind of physical and emotional reaction to what you've sent, it strengthens your bond.

One of my favorite cartoons is shown below. I like this cartoon because virtually anyone can relate to it. It has worked well for me in the approach process because "never" is often the only time the prospect/client is free to meet.

"No, Thursday's out. How about never—is never good for you?"

 ### Use Cartoons Correctly

Cartoons used as a marketing tool have to make sense. They must relate to what it is you are connecting with this person about. Also, they cannot in any way be offensive. And copyright must be adhered to.

Visibility Venue #7:
Promotional Premiums

Promotional premiums work best when they are not only of good quality, but also of good use and value to the recipient. For example, if I receive another free mouse pad in the mail from a vendor, I'm going to scream! This premium does not excite me. It adds clutter to my work space, and I already have a perfectly fine mouse pad: black, with no promo writing on it.

That's not to say that this type of premium may not be effective or useful, because in the right market it might be well-received. The key is to keep your target market in mind when selecting your promotion premiums.

Protect Your Image!

Promotion premiums are tricky. You want to stay visible, yet everything you send with your name on it reflects back on you. Are your premiums sophisticated; useful; shoddy; or gimmicky? Do they consistently convey the high quality that you represent in the way you do business? Find a promotion premium firm that will work closely with you to convey the best message for your business.

Evaluating Your Promotion Premiums

To determine what to send, ask the following:

- "What message does this send?"
- "How will they react upon receiving it?"
- "Will they keep it or toss it?"
- "How will they improve themselves by using it?"

Visibility Venue #8: Announcements

Announcements can be a subtle and dignified way to keep a high profile, if they are done in the right manner. You can make announcements in local publications regarding your own promotion, the promotion of someone in your organization, the introduction of a new product, or even the opening of a new office. My favorite, though, is announcing that a new client has selected us as a business partner. I once saw this concept used very effectively by an architectural firm. The announcement read as follows:

We are delighted to announce that Bromley Corporation has selected our firm to design their international headquarters in Zurich, Switzerland.

This announcement was sent in the form of a mailing to everyone in the company's database. It was printed on the finest paper. The shape of the card was 4 × 4 inches, another attention-getter (square-shaped cards are a great clutter-buster), and it used as few words as possible. It signaled how proud the firm was to have another high-quality client join its long-established list of clients.

The beauty of this type of promotion is that it keeps prospects and customers informed of the new and prestigious clients you are acquiring.

Your Competition Is Always Watching

It is necessary to use some caution when making announcements. Some information is not for public consumption. For example, sometimes it may be a mistake to announce a new client coming aboard. It can become a quick target for your competition.

Visibility Venue #9: Outrageous Stuff

Sometimes being creative is the best way to cut through the clutter. Here are some instances of outrageous attention-getters: A client of mine said when he was in entry-level sales he used to cold-call a lot as part of the door-to-door selling of his company's telecommunication services. At first he received tons of rejection and felt he wasn't making any progress.

Then he decided to staple a small bag of M&M's to his business card when leaving it with the receptionist. He said he got a positive response from this. Also, contacts to whom he gave his card directly seemed to appreciate the sugar boost. When following up by telephone, people he had not seen but had left a card for knew immediately who he was as soon as he said that his card was the one with the M&Ms. More often than not, this attention-getting visibility tactic worked in his favor.

Another unusual marketing tool this client used when selling was a cake. On rare occasions toward the end of the decision-making process, he would send the prospect a cake. The icing would read: "Some Decisions Are Hard To Make, This One Is A Piece Of Cake." More often than not he would get a return phone call.

One novel success story involved an advertising account executive from a running magazine who was wooing a luxury automobile company. After countless attempts to get the decision maker's attention, the account executive started to befriend the decision maker's secretary. Then one day, they started to brainstorm ideas on how the sales rep could make contact. A new brand of Nikes had just come out, and the secretary suggested that sending a pair of the running shoes as a gift might help. The sales professional did not feel comfortable "buying" her way in. But she decided that if she sent only one shoe, she might get the return call and meeting she was seeking.

She asked the secretary for the decision maker's shoe size. Then she mailed him one Nike running shoe, with a note that read: "Now that I have one foot in the door, please help me get the other one in. I have an idea to share with you that will increase sales. Please give me a call." Do you think he called? Yes! If for nothing else but to get that other shoe. And once he heard her pitch, he decided to give it a try.

This technique for enhancing visibility probably has a higher potential for backfiring than less extreme visibility techniques. But hey, have you ever targeted a prospect/client that you were confident could benefit enormously from what you had to offer, yet you just could not get through? No matter how hard you tried? If you have nothing, you have nothing to lose. Think it through. Take the risk and track the results.

> When nothing is sure, everything is possible.
> *Margaret Drabble*

 ### Watch It

It is of critical importance to keep in mind that tactics like those just cited do not always work. Also, they involve a certain level of risk-taking. It is necessary to think of a way to get your prospect's/client's attention that is creative yet acceptable, without being viewed as a turn-off.

Check in with someone you know who works closely with the decision maker. This person—who is typically called an "inside coach" or "influencer"—can provide insight as to what kinds of outrageous stuff will be well-received.

Visibility Venue #10: Association Events/Networking Functions

As discussed in Chapter 3, getting out and networking at association events and functions is crucial. Every point of human contact brings you that much closer to a sale. And, the way you come across to the public is of vital importance. Preparing your introduction in advance allows you to present yourself in a good light.

Mark Twain said that it took him about three hours to prepare a really good, spontaneous one-minute speech. Maybe that's why he is still so widely quoted today.

Prepare Your "30-Second Introduction"

When you know you will be going to an association event, prepare your opening statement, or 30-second introduction. Then prepare and rehearse, and prepare and rehearse, until it no longer sounds prepared and rehearsed. Know exactly what you need to say about what you do, in 30 seconds or less. Also, try to think of an interesting or creative way to introduce yourself besides the standard, "Hi, my name is . . . and I do . . ." (Boring!)

Three years ago I was at a networking meeting in California. It was a very foggy and rainy morning, and we were all a little tired as we went around the room doing our rote introductions. The meeting was in a banquet hall with a public address system that kept announcing license plate numbers of cars in the parking lot whose headlights had been left on.

In the meeting, the next person who stood up to introduce himself said, "I have a brief announcement to make to the person with the yellow Yugo out in the parking lot. I didn't want you to run your battery down, so I smashed in your headlights. Hi, I'm John Kinde, and I am a humor consultant." Then he sat down. That 30-second introduction got full audience attention and probably generated more business prospects than did any other speaker's presentation that day. Moreover, I still remember it clearly today. Okay, so we are not all in the humor business, but we still know how to laugh and recognize things that are funny. If you take some time to add a little humor to your introduction or presentation you may find that it allows for quicker and stronger connections to be made. A touch of humor is well worth the effort.

Visibility Venue #11: Trade Shows

Trade shows were mentioned earlier in this chapter, as an excellent way to find business. They also are a great way for you and your company to stay visible.

While attending a trade show, enhance your visibility by:

- Walking around
- Smiling
- Energetically introducing yourself
- Attending on-site seminars
- Volunteering to help out at the trade show
- Making a positive and determined effort to connect with others
- Preparing your compelling 30-second introduction

Enhance your company's visibility by:

- Exhibiting a booth
- Sponsoring a cocktail hour
- Conducting a seminar
- Displaying a banner
- Providing useful premiums
- Providing an interactive experience for those who enter your booth

Visibility Venue #12: The "Pop-In"

Many highly successful sales professionals at a variety of levels of experience feel that the "pop-in" approach works very well. The "pop-in" approach entails dropping by, unannounced, to touch base, to deliver a proposal, to discuss how things are going, to drop off some relevant material. The act of stopping by can be hit-or-miss, but it shows you took the time out of your busy day to do something for your prospect/client.

Recently I spoke to a very high level sales executive who told me she uses the pop-in all the time and finds it highly effective. She said, "Sometimes people would never expect me to just pop in to see them. It adds an element of surprise in many ways: They are surprised that it is not beneath me to pop in; it shows that I'm thinking of them; and when I schlep stuff over to their office, the intimidation barrier is broken because they think, "Wow, she's doing this for me!"

Take the Company Tour

Another way to stay visible is to ask for a company tour. You get to become better acquainted with the company and many people in the organization get to see you.

DANGER!

The Pop-in Drawback

One of the few drawbacks to the pop-in approach is if you have a prospect/client who would find an unannounced visit annoying. But in most cases the response is one of gratitude. You also get a chance to meet face-to-face again, which is the best type of visibility, and in most cases it strengthens the relationship.

KEEP CONNECTING

Self-managed selling thrives when you have the discipline to continually focus on the connection process. That's what it's all about—who to call, what to say, how to keep in touch, and always how to close the deal!

Selling Better

The Exceptional Preparation Process

Before everything else, getting ready is the secret of success.

anonymous

Adequate preparation for sales calls is of critical importance to being a successful self-managed sales professional. Yet, many salespeople do not take the time to properly prepare. "Winging it" is a common occurrence. Despite the fact that sales professionals tend to be risk-takers, winging it is one risk that should be avoided.

The preparation process can be a painless one. The benefits of preparation are great; these include building confidence, exuding credibility, reducing nervousness, and increasing sales revenue. This chapter will detail the following concepts:

- The structure of the preparation process
- Customer-focused planning
- Preparing to involve your customer
- Questioning choreography
- Preparing to listen
- The satisfaction continuum
- Uncovering the objections
- "Next-step" selling

KEY CONCEPT — THE STRUCTURE OF THE PREPARATION PROCESS

One simple yet highly effective technique for sales call planning is the "Before, During, and After" process, also referred to as the *BDA Strategy.*™ The BDA Strategy allows for the self-managed sales professional to think of the sales call in terms of three stages:

- The Before Stage—anticipating what can be done before walking in the door to assure that the meeting will result in a sale at best, or a return visit at worst

- The During Stage—determining what can be done in the meeting to gain and sustain the prospect's/client's interest, and to move the meeting in the direction of a tangible sale versus just a pleasant social call

- The After Stage—planning ahead what action to take once the meeting has ended

Let's explore all three stages of the BDA planning process in more depth. And use these suggestions as checklists before, during, and after the sales call.

The Before Stage

Fifteen of the activities you can consider doing in this stage are as follows:

- ☑ Write down the questions you will be asking on this sales call. (See more on choreographing questions later in this chapter.)

- ☑ Research the company, using the Internet, your database, records of past history, annual reports, infotrack software, and so forth.

- ☑ Gather all of your sales promotional material and put it in the order you plan to use it on the sales call.

- ☑ Know your competition and why you and your company are different and better than the rest.

- ☑ Bring show-and-tell items like testimonial letters, pertinent cartoons, an obscure piece of your product for the client to touch and guess where it fits into the big picture.

- ☑ Anticipate objections. List all of the probable ones and prepare comebacks for each.

- ☑ Create an agenda. If appropriate, fax/mail/ e-mail a copy to your contact person.

- ☑ Think of how to immediately engage the prospect/client through the use of questions, stories, or analogies that invite involvement.

- ☑ Plan the opening and closing statements of your presentation thoroughly.
- ☑ Troubleshoot technology: Charge batteries, bring back-up batteries and bulbs, and so forth.
- ☑ Envision your success.
- ☑ Prepare to arrive 15 minutes before the meeting.
- ☑ Get very specific directions (cross-street, floor number, etc.) to the meeting place.
- ☑ Use your power word/phrase to control nervousness (See Chapter 3).
- ☑ Relax and breathe!

Prepare Thoroughly

Thorough preparation is one of the secrets to effective negotiation. By giving yourself more time than usual in the Before stage of the BDA process you will be creating a solid foundation that will increase your likelihood of success.

Get Out There!

Be careful not to spend so much time on preparation that you lose sight of the big picture, which is having as many quality face-to-face client encounters as possible and obtaining the right to go to the next step in the relationship. Keep in mind that if Woody Allen is correct when he says that 80 percent of success is just showing up, then, showing up *prepared* should increase that success rate to over 90 percent!

The During Stage

Here are 20 activities that you can consider doing in this stage:

- ☑ Arrive early.
- ☑ Befriend the decision maker's receptionist and assistants.
- ☑ State the purpose of the meeting and verify agreement.
- ☑ Get the prospect involved!
- ☑ Ask questions, tell stories, give analogies, bring show-and-tell items.
- ☑ Use your powerful opening and closing statements.

- ☑ Ask for a company tour.
- ☑ Align your products/service with the prospect/client's need.
- ☑ Uncover possible objections.
- ☑ Build rapport, discover common interests.
- ☑ Gain client commitment.
- ☑ Close. Ask for the business or at least the next step.
- ☑ Ask for internal or external referrals.
- ☑ Allow yourself an extra margin when making time commitments (such as when a proposal will be ready), so that you can keep your promises and honor those commitments.
- ☑ Summarize what was covered in the meeting and the action steps to follow.
- ☑ Check for acknowledgment of the summary and action steps.
- ☑ Discuss timeframe to fulfill commitments.
- ☑ Lock in a date on your calendar to come back for a follow-up meeting!
- ☑ Leave with a warm smile and solid, confident handshake.
- ☑ Remember your friendly "good-byes" to the secretaries and receptionists.

The After Stage

Eight activities that you can consider putting into action in this stage are as follows:

- ☑ Self-evaluate: Think over, or write down the answers to the following self-evaluation questions after you leave the meeting/sales call:

1. What did I do that worked?
2. What did I do that could be improved?
3. What will I do in the future to make it a better sales call?

- ☑ Now ask yourself a different set of questions:

1. What did I like about the sales call?
2. What did I learn?
3. What would I change?

- ☑ Review your notes and fill in any sketchy areas.
- ☑ Update database.

☑ Keep your promises!

☑ Plan to underpromise and overdeliver: Honor promises made, ahead of schedule.

☑ Follow-up and keep in close touch.

☑ Call any referrals received within 24 hours of the meeting.

☑ Prepare for your next meeting.

KEY CONCEPT — CUSTOMER-FOCUSED PLANNING

Your prospect/customer will listen longer and be more apt to make a commitment to you if you prepare a customer-focused presentation. You are probably well aware of the age-old acronym for being customer-focused: WIIFM. WIIFM stands for *"What's In It For Me?"* As another way to remember it, some people refer to this acronym as "the favorite radio station" of your prospect/customer, "W.I.I. on your F.M. dial." Yet another mnemonic device for this concept is "The WIIFM cloud"—meaning, surround your customer in the WIIFM cloud and you will gain more sales.

Why are there so many mnemonic devices for this concept? Because it is one of the most important concepts for sales professionals to remember, yet so often the first one forgotten. Think of how overwhelming the professional sales process can be with all of the preparation, execution, follow-through, and multitude of details that need to be taken care of, and you will see how easy it is to lose sight of the essential, basic concept of staying customer-focused.

Sometimes sales professionals may even think that they are being totally customer-focused as they spew out all of their FAB statements (FAB: "Feature, Advantage, Benefit"—)and yet they are staying in the comfort zone of routine. Often a routine of the "spray and pray" variety! Spray out a plethora of research, data, and focus group studies to your prospect/customer, and pray that something sticks. The real strategy for customer-focused selling is to ask questions, listen intently, and then solve the customer's problems with your product/service.

How time flies when you are doing all the talking.
Harvey Fierstein.

Do Investigative Work First

Customer-focused planning also involves some investigative work. Call someone in the organization from whom you might be able to obtain some information about your contact. Ask what products/services have been used in the past and, if possible, what his or her attitude is toward what you are selling. You can also do this directly with the contact if you feel comfortable. The more you can learn about the prospect/customer before the sales call, the better your chances are of being on target during the call.

No Interrogations, Please

Be careful about sounding too interrogative with insiders who you do not know very well. Recently I was on a sales call when I discovered that my contact's assistant was his mother! (I discovered this fact later when I was complimenting the contact on the professionalism of his administrative assistant.) Yes, in all-sized companies all kinds of relationships can occur and you have to be diplomatic about what you ask and how you ask it.

Keep the Respect

Remember to keep in mind the "Make Me Feel Important" philosophy of rapport building. It essentially means that most people like to be treated with respect. If you find a sincere way to give a compliment, or a genuine way to convey that you find the contact's background or company impressive (when indeed you do), you will strengthen the bond between the two of you.

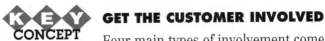

GET THE CUSTOMER INVOLVED

Four main types of involvement come to mind regarding staying customer-focused: (1) questions; (2) stories, (3) analogies, and (4) show-and-tell items. Let's cover each in turn.

Questions

Preparing questions prior to the sales call and steadily asking them throughout the meeting is probably the best way to keep your prospect/customer involved, while simultaneously identifying his or her core needs.

For example, the following question can be very powerful: "What is most important to you about . . . ?" This question works well because it seeks a need without bluntly asking, "So, what are your needs?" It provides a more subtle, sophisticated approach.

DANGER!

Dig Deeper

Be careful not to take the first answer to this question as the real answer. Why? Because asking this type of question usually helps your prospect to think of the first thing on his/her mind but doesn't allow for deeper thinking.

TiP

Ask "Chaser" Questions

After the question, "What is most important to you about . . . ?" it's important to follow up with two "chaser" questions, such as, "Why is that?" and "Is there anything else?" These chaser questions help the prospect/customer to think about his or her true need on a deeper level. Once he or she has mentioned a few responses to your first question and chaser questions, summarize and prioritize his/her response. In doing this you are helping your prospect/customer to *think*, which is one of the most important jobs of a true sales consultant.

Deeper Involvement Questions

"How do you feel about . . . ?" and "What is your opinion of . . . ?" types of questions help to build rapport by allowing your prospect/customer to state his or her view on key issues.

When does anyone really have the time or opportunity to share their opinions any more anyway?! Many business professionals seem to be far too busy. This line of questioning also serves as a way to make your prospect/client feel important. People feel valued when asked to express their thoughts and opinions. Just be sure to be sincere.

Involvement questions that help you to uncover any possible obstacles to your sale are as follows: "Is there anything that would prevent you from working with us?" or the more direct: "What might prevent you from working with us?" They also help the prospect/customer troubleshoot obstacles that may stand in the way of you doing business together. Some sales professionals are

GET THE SKINNY — FIND out your opponents plan — where do you fit into his life?

afraid to ask these types of questions. They don't want to risk planting a seed of doubt in the prospect's/customer's mind. But in many cases, without an objection, you don't get a sale. (More on objection handling in Chapter 6.)

"Describe how you would picture . . ." or "What would your ideal . . . be?" Allow your prospect/customer to dream. In many cases you can make dreams come true. And even if you can't, you have taken your relationship to a different level by asking about a "dream goal."

Stories

Preparing stories to tell about how your organization has helped its customers grow and prosper is a useful and highly effective involvement technique. Many times people would much rather hear what *others* think or have experienced versus what *you* think or have experienced. A third-party story is a great way to provide information, sell yourself, and positively promote your product/service. It is helpful to bring a letter of recommendation (also referred to as a "testimonial" letter) on the sales call to make the story more believable.

Analogies

When you can make comparisons it makes it easier for the customer to see the value of what you are saying. You're describing something in a different way, which may have a greater impact.

Show-and-Tell

A show-and-tell item involves the salesperson bringing in a tangible yet unusual piece of the product or service that is being sold. One sales professional said that when selling long-distance telephone service it was difficult to gain the client's interest for two main reasons: Being a service, it was hard to actually see it; and long-distance telephone service sales professionals were everywhere, making for a crowded field.

To make the presentation a little more interesting, the sales professional brought a piece of telephone cable with him on the sales call, along with some fiber optic thread to "show-and-tell." He found that this technique immediately changed the mood and tone of the sales call. He was no longer perceived or treated like "just another long-distance sales guy."

BOTTOM LINE **Customer Involvement Works**

Customer involvement rules! It rocks. It gets results.

KEY CONCEPT — PREPARE OPEN-ENDED AND CLOSED-ENDED QUESTIONS

In addition to the involvement questions previously mentioned in this chapter, it is essential that you prepare a list of different types of questions that will build upon each other and guide the direction and outcome of the meeting.

Once you have written down a list of questions to ask, it is helpful to put them into an order that both makes sense to the flow of conversation and leads to an appropriate series of closing questions.

When generating questions prior to a sales call, keep in mind that there are two main types of questions (and many subtypes) that can be formulated. The two main types are the *open-ended question* and the *closed-ended question*.

Open-Ended Questions

The open-ended question opens up a conversation. It starts with words and phrases such as, "How would you describe . . . ?" "What is your opinion of . . . ?" "How do you feel about . . . ?" What would be your ideal scenario?" "What do you like most about our product/service?" These types of questions yield a lot of information. They are used as a way to get your prospect/customer talking.

Let Your Client Speak!

The Golden Rule in effective self-managed selling is that the sales professional speaks 20 percent of the time in the sales meeting and the client prospect speaks 80 percent or more of the time. One way to achieve this balance is by asking open-ended questions and using silence to allow your prospect/customer to speak. By choreographing questions so that your prospect/customer speaks more than you do, you will be more likely to gain knowledge that will further the sale and less likely to say something that might turn off the client.

Wisdom is the reward you get for a lifetime of listening when you'd have preferred to talk.

anonymous

If you can't be quiet, shut up!
anonymous

Tell Me!

The "Tell Me" technique is another great way to open up conversation. An example would be, "Tell me, how did you . . . ?" "Tell me your thoughts on . . ." The "Tell Me" technique acts more as a command than a question, but it is said in a way that is unobtrusive when used correctly. The "Tell Me" technique provides as much information as most open-ended questions do.

DANGER!

Avoid Answering Your Own Question!

When preparing your questions, write yourself a note not to answer your own question. It's a common habit, and you need to avoid it. You won't receive the best information if you attempt to fill in answers for your customer. Also, by listening instead of speaking you'll save yourself the embarrassment or filling the silence with the wrong answer.

Closed-Ended Questions

The second main type of questions to formulate prior to your sales call are closed-ended questions. Closed-ended questions typically yield one-word, "yes" or "no" answers. The words and phrases most often used when creating closed-ended questions are: "Do you?" "Are you?" "Have you?" "Will you?" "Can you?" "Is there?" Examples of closed-ended questions would be: "Can you see how our product would be beneficial for you to use?" "Are you interested in our service as a solution to your core issues?" "Do you have any other RFPs (requests for proposals) back yet?" Have you met with any other vendors yet?" "Are you planning to . . . ?" "Is there anything that would prevent us from working together?"

Just as open-ended questions open up a conversation, closed-ended questions close the conversation down. They cut-to-the-chase and are very direct.

Both open and closed-ended questions are important to prepare before your meeting.

Avoid an Interrogation!

Many sales professionals make the mistake of not writing down key questions and practicing them before a meeting. They tend to wing it. The problem with winging it is that most people ask too many closed-ended questions when speaking impromptu. By asking "Do you?" . . . "Are you?" . . . "Have you?" your prospect/customer will respond "yes," "no," "yes," "no," "no," "yes." Not only does this line of questioning prevent the prospect/client from speaking the necessary 80 percent of the time, but you'll begin to sound like you're interrogating, not consulting.

PREPARE TO TAKE THE LEAD

To "choreograph" means to arrange, and this term is usually applied to a dance. In successful sales calls a sort of dance also happens, and it's up to the self-managed sales professional to take the lead in that dance.

One of the best ways to do this is by arranging both open-ended and closed-ended questions before the sales call, and practicing using them in different ways for different purposes. A few examples of choreographing open-ended and closed-ended questions are as follows:

"It's nice to see you again. How have you been?" (Closed-ended.) "What technology have you been using since we last met?" (Closed-ended.) "Tell me what your experience has been with it?" (Open-ended.) "What changes would you like to see?" (Open-ended.) "How might I be able to assist you with those changes?" (Open-ended.) "What time frame did you have in mind?" (Closed-ended.) "When do you think we could get started on this?" (Closed-ended.) "When can we meet again to move toward the next step?" (Closed-ended.)

"Who in addition to yourself, will be in on the decision-making process?" (Open-ended.) Versus, "Is there anyone else who will be involved in this decision-making process?" (Closed-ended.) "What else do I need to know?" (Open-ended.) Versus, "Is there anything else I need to know?" (Closed-ended.)

Interject Interest

Plan on interjecting phrases that convey your interest and enthusiasm during the sales call.

I once went on a sales call with a top-producing sales professional. I was there to evaluate the effectiveness of the call. I wrote down the questions the sales person was asking, along with the responses interjected by the prospect during the conversation. The sales professional's side of the conversation went like this:

"Good morning. It's nice to meet you. I know we have only a few minutes to meet. Thanks for fitting me into your schedule today. The purpose of this meeting is to familiarize you briefly with our organization as well as to determine how you might be able to benefit from using our services; and, finally, to talk about the logical next step. Does that make sense to you?" (Closed-ended checking/involvement question.) "We do . . . (one-minute description of what we do). What is most important to you about . . . ?" (Open-ended.) "Why is that?" (Open-ended chaser.) "Is there anything else?" (Closed-ended chaser.) "Why is that?" (Open-ended chaser.) "Uh huh, uh huh, uh huh, really? Wow, tell me more." (Open-ended command.)

OTHER TYPES OF QUESTIONS TO PREPARE FOR AND CHOREOGRAPH

Chaser Questions

As mentioned earlier in this chapter, chaser questions can be added on to your original questions to draw out the most important information. Some examples are: "Why is that?" "Anything else?" "What other methods do you see?"

Checking Questions

Checking questions are questions that verify the true meaning of what was said and also seek to confirm the communication. Examples: "Does this make sense to you?" . . . "Is this what you're looking for?" . . . "Do you agree that . . . ?" When asking a checking question you are actually forming a bilateral verbal contract of agreement. This type of questioning can strengthen commitment and assure more active listening. (More on "preparing to listen" later in this chapter.)

Hypothetical Questions

These are questions that help the prospect/customer think about possibilities. Examples of hypothetical questions are:

- "What if there were no budgetary constraints. What would your ideal program be?"
- "What if we were able to have some flexibility, what would you see us doing here?"

Hypothetical questions usually start off with the phrase "What if . . ." or the word "Suppose." Such as: "Suppose we could . . . how might that effect your decision?"

Hypothetical questioning can stimulate "out-of-the-box" thinking. It places proposed ideas and options into a conversational "dream-machine." The smart thing to do then is to take the information back to your office and think of creative ways to turn these brainstormed dreams into solid reality.

By dreaming with your prospects/customers you'll increase the probability of fulfilling their needs. But on the flip side, be careful not to get too excited and promise something you'll have to renegotiate later.

Closing Questions

Closing questions are questions that allow you to advance to the next step in the process toward closure, or, allow you to actually close the deal, depending on where you are in the sales cycle. Examples of some closing questions are as follows:

- "How do you feel about this product/service?" (Open-ended.)
- "Can you see this product/service working for you?" (Closed-ended.)
- "What are the steps necessary to move ahead at this time?" (Open-ended.)
- "What is your interest level, on a scale of 1 to 10?" (Closed-ended.) "What would make it a 10?" (Open-ended.)
- "What is the logical next step?" (Open-ended.)
- "Is there anything that might prevent us from moving forward?" (Closed-ended.) "What might that be?" (Open-ended.)

As you can see from this sample list of closing questions, careful planning and rehearsing are necessary to decide which questions to ask at each stage of the sales process. Intelligent choice and sequencing of the open-ended, closed-ended, chaser, checking, hypothetical, and closing questions are essential for success in leading your prospect/customer toward and finally committing to buy your product/service.

BOTTOM LINE **Planning Matters**

"Winging it" is for the birds!

KEY CONCEPT **PREPARE TO LISTEN**

Listening is a skill. It takes time, patience, and keen awareness to perfect. Many view listening as synonymous with hearing, but it is not. Hearing is a physiological mechanical function of picking up sound. Listening is much more of an active, conscious mental or cognitive skill that attends to the meaning of the message being sent.

Because listening is a skill, it takes practice to refine. The best part about practicing to listen is that you can do it just about anywhere. If you set a goal to listen intently at home, with friends and family, en route to sales calls, in small talk with taxi drivers and in the office or on the phone with colleagues, you will have a head start toward improving your ability to listen on sales calls.

In the communication process, as any Communications 101 class will tell you, there is a sender and a receiver of every message, and interference or "noise" in the process is the greatest cause of miscommunication.

In business communications, especially in selling, interference is usually found in the form of distractions. Therefore, effective listening takes a great deal of practice primarily because distractions are so abundant. There are two main types of distractions: (1) internal distractions, and (2) external distractions. Let's explore each type.

Internal Distractions

These are distractions that occur within your mind. They are the thoughts that pop into your head as someone is speaking to you that interfere with fully and accurately receiving the sender's message.

Why does this internal interference occur? Because your mind can think at approximately 500 to 600 or more words per minute (w.p.m.), while most people only speak at a rate of 100 to 125 words per minute, with bursts of up to 150 per minute if they speak very quickly. The fastest speakers in the world—the *Guinness Book of World Records* variety—can talk in the 300+ words-per-minute range. Obviously, if you blasted your client/prospect at that speed, he or she would be distracted. However, a slow, ponderous presentation can also lose out. The challenge is to develop through practice a versatile range of speech based on your optimum thinking and talking speeds.

With the potentially wide gap between the w.p.m. rate at which people speak and the w.p.m. rate at which they think, no wonder our minds wander and we lose our concentration. To overcome a wandering mind, learn to identify points of interest in the conversation.

Identify Points of Interest

A formula to keep in mind when working toward becoming a better listener is: concentration equals interest versus distraction. This means that if you are interested enough in what is being said, you will attend to the message more keenly—regardless of any internal or external distractions.

But what if the message is not compelling? What if the prospect/client is rambling on about something and you lose your concentration? You need to take control and do something to get back on track. Ask a question that will get you and your prospect/client focused on the purpose of your meeting.

The opposite of talking isn't listening. The opposite of talking is waiting.
Fran Lebowitz

External Distractions

These are the distractions that occur in the environment you happen to be in. Examples include the telephone ringing; an e-mail bing; or a siren from a passing ambulance. External distractions are often unpredictable; to recover from them you to expect that at some point they will happen, and when they do, focus on tuning them out making a commitment to attend to what your customer is saying.

THE SATISFACTION CONTINUUM

CONCEPT

Another important part of the preparation process is preparing the satisfaction continuum. The satisfaction continuum is typically measured on a scale of 1 to 10 (with 10 being the most satisfied and 1 the least). To effectively use this continuum, ask yourself a few key questions such as, "What do I want to accomplish on this sales call?" It is critical to anticipate the degree of satisfaction—yours as well as the prospect's—before going on a sales call. Then make a list of everything that you want without any reservation. In essence you are compiling a list of items that would give you a "10" rating on your continuum. Then, repeat this same activity, but from the customer's point of view, asking "What are all the things the customer would want to get from me that would rate a "10" on his or her continuum?"

Go the extra mile to deliberately have your customer WIN!

Of course it is not always possible to win the lottery by scoring a 10 on your desired outcome continuum by the end of your meeting. Therefore, you also need to make a list of concessions. You might ask yourself, "What am I willing to give up in order for this sale to work?" Or the flip side: "What might the customer be willing to do without or to give up?"

Prioritize the items on both lists and determine a variety of ways to achieve win/win satisfaction. For instance, if your client's satisfaction regarding an outcome is a 9 on his or her continuum but only a 4 on yours, you need to reevaluate your strategy.

Seek True Wants and Needs

Connect with someone in the organization who has a good understanding of your customer's wants and needs and is willing to share them with you. This type of research will help you formulate a win/win strategy. Mutual benefit yields mutual respect—a key ingredient in any successful business relationship. Be careful to seek a win/win outcome, by not giving too much.

114

 **PREPARING TO UNCOVER**
THE OBJECTIONS

It is amazing how many sales professionals get thrown off by the same customer objections over and over again, call after call. But there's a simple solution for this. It is to be aware that there are typically six to eight objections that come up over and over again on sales calls. If you can anticipate what these objections are and prepare an abundance of comebacks for each, you will reduce the anxiety and fear so often associated with prospect/customer objections. You will also feel more confident, and possibly even welcome challenging objection questions, as you discover that objections from prospects and customers are in many cases an indication of interest.

So what are some typical objections? Money is usually the first one that comes to mind. Are your products or services the highest-priced ones in your industry? Maybe so, but that's because you represent high-quality service and deal with people who value quality.

Some strategies for answering "Your price is too high" include:

- "Well, let's revisit why you are interested in working with us. You said you were interested in obtaining X results and the value to you would be Y. Is that right? To deliver X, we need to charge Z."

- "We have a certain pricing model we use which is how we determine our fees." "What part of the product/service would you want eliminated to justify a lower fee?"

- "Flinch" by acting surprised that the prospect/customer feels that way by saying, "Really?! What makes you feel that our price is too high?"

It will be a wise investment of your time to seek to anticipate and troubleshoot every conceivable objection before making your sales call. By doing so you can expect increasingly successful sales calls and meetings and far less anxiety.

In addition to price, other common objections may be: You are not on our approved vendor list; We are happy with our current supplier; We had a bad experience with you before.

Some comebacks would be:

- "How do I get on your approved vendor list?"
- "Some of my clients who were originally happy with their current supplier used me as a backup vendor initially."
- "What can I do to make it up to you? I'm willing to work this through."

One door opens, another door closes.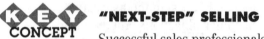
Helen Keller

"NEXT-STEP" SELLING

KEY CONCEPT

Successful sales professionals are constantly thinking of the next step in the sales process.

"Next-step" selling focuses on proceeding to a further level after every sales call. To do this begin with the end in mind. Where do you want this meeting to take you? To the next meeting? And who will be in that next meeting? To a referral? How would you use that referral to increase business? To the proposal stage? When will you come back to go over that proposal?

Next-step selling involves being focused on your mission and your specific objectives as well as discovering how to gain permission to proceed to that next step without appearing too "pushy" or aggressive. Here are a few useful phrases to keep in mind:

- "So, to summarize the key points of this meeting: First, you are looking for X, Y, and Z. Is that right?" (Checking question.) "What would be the logical next step? Can we set up the next step on the calendar now?"
- "Based on this conversation, I am highly confident that I can assist you in providing the highest quality service for your ____, how do you feel?" (Checking question.)

If you feel that the prospect/customer feels quite positively about the service, possibly continue with . . . "So when can we meet again?"

- "So, where do we go from here?"
- "Who, in addition to yourself, will be involved in the decision-making process? When might I meet him or her?"
- "What other divisions might benefit from being aware of our services? Who might I call?"

- "Can you give me some rough, ballpark idea of the next steps involved in your own decision-making process?" (Days, weeks, months?)
- "When would be the best time for me to follow up?"
- "When should I touch base with you?"
- "Can we schedule a follow-up conference call? When would be the best day and time for you?"
- "When do you think you might be able to make a commitment?"
- "If at some time in the future you were to go ahead, would you prefer (*this*) or (*this*)?

With the "next-step" selling technique, you'll zero in on the best way to proceed in the sales process. One of the biggest downfalls of many sales professionals is that they dance around the close. The end of the sales call becomes awkward. The words to further the sale are hard to come by. Most salespeople end their meeting with the weak (if not whimpering, or whiny) phrase, "So what do you think?" This is not a closing question. More often than not a closing question contains the word "when."

BOTTOM LINE **"When" Is the Key Word to the Close**

Say "when"—as in "When do you think you'll have a decision?" Getting to "when" gets you closer to the sale.

SETTING THE FOUNDATION FOR SUCCESS

Preparation lays the foundation for successful sales results. By planning the structure of your call, as well as anticipating the use of customer-focused planning, involvement, questioning, listening, a satisfaction continuum, responding to objections, and the next-step technique, you'll be on the path to successful results.

Conducting Persuasive, Results-Driven Sales Calls

All things come to those who go after them.
Rob Estes

By the time you have gone through all of the effort (and at times, agony) required to achieve the scheduling of a sales call, you will also want to be sure you've done everything possible toward walking away from that meeting one step closer to gaining the sale. In this chapter you will discover a variety of valuable sales techniques that, when implemented, will assist you in obtaining the results you are seeking. Chapter 5 was geared toward preparation for the sales call; in Chapter 6 we will be focusing on detailed implementation of that plan.

IMPLEMENTING THE STRUCTURE

When conducting a sales call, you must act as a leader. You decide how to orchestrate the sales meeting. One powerful and highly effective approach is to plan *three* key points to focus on. Three has been proven to be a magic number when making a presentation; usually one or two points are too few to sell an idea, and four or more are too many for the prospect/customer to grasp. Three points are also effective because that many are the easiest to remember.

Even the Romans felt that three was ideal; they coined the phrase *trinum perfectum est,* meaning "three is perfect."

One of the best and simplest presentation models is a technique called *threefold and verify*. The way it works is that you begin your meeting by explaining that its purpose is threefold. "First, I'll bring you up to speed on some of the new technologies we've been developing. Second, we will explore your specific interests in learning how we can help provide business solutions for you and your company. And third, we can talk about the next step—where we go from here." And then you verify by saying, "Does this make sense to you?"

To summarize the threefold and verify, you are essentially setting up the meeting agenda. You will be discussing (1) you, (2) them, and (3) the next step. Depending on how you want to structure the meeting, you could also reverse this order and talk about (1) them, (2) you, and (3) the next step.

Keep the Meeting's Focus on Your Customer More than on Yourself

Be careful when you get to the "you" step of the conversation. You'll want to stay customer-focused by spending as little time as possible talking about yourself and the majority of the meeting time talking about "them."

One of the beauties of the threefold and verify technique is that it sets up "the close" in the first few seconds of the conversation by stating, "and third, we'll talk about the next step." You are setting the expectation that you will be asking for permission to proceed to the next step. And by asking the verifying question, "Does that make sense?" you are gaining commitment that it is okay for you to close.

The threefold and verify allows you to put your thoughts and sales information into a clear and structured format. (Many salespeople are "people" people and tend to be weak regarding structure.) It also makes "the close" less awkward because it is expected and agreed to up front.

Watch Your Language!

The threefold and verify technique when used in "textbook fashion" can sound very formal (i.e., "The purpose of this meeting is . . .") If you find this wording too stuffy-sounding or canned, you can change the wording while keeping the same structure. A more casual, "familiar" approach would be to say, "I thought we could discuss three areas today." Or, "I've planned three main topics to go over today." The key is to use language that you are comfortable with.

The definition of a good presentation: a good beginning, a good ending, and preferably close together.

Anonymous

KEY CONCEPT — IMPLEMENTING CUSTOMER-FOCUSED SELLING

In addition to keeping in mind WIIFM ("What's In It For Me?") on your sales calls, it's important to use techniques to stay in tune with your customer. The three main areas to focus your time and attention are (1) rapport building; (2) personality evaluating; and (3) body language imaging. Let's look at these in turn.

Rapport Building

The key to effective rapport building is to be observant. When you begin a sales call it is important for you to be aware of environmental cues that will provide some insights into the "person" behind the prospect/customer. The photos on the desk, the pictures on the wall, and the awards on the shelves all have meaning and value to that individual. By observing these items and asking questions or making comments about them, you will learn more about your prospect/customer.

When I walked into a customer's office recently, the first thing I noticed was a large picture of a race car on the wall, and I asked if he drove race cars. It turned out that he did and was in the process of restoring one in his garage. This information enabled me to add a more human element to that and subsequent meetings by asking how he was progressing with his endless race car restoration project.

It might seem cliché to ask about the "wife/husband and kids," but many times people do like to talk about them, and doing so does build rapport.

Don't Get Off-Course

When building rapport be careful that you don't get caught up in a long-winded conversation that deflects you from your goal. Some people tend to go on at great length about their personal lives and interests. It is up to you, as the sales professional, to gently guide the conversation back on course.

The second area of customer-focused selling to be aware of is personality evaluating. Insight is the key here. By having an insight as to what personality traits you possess, and being able to observe and determine the traits of others, you will be able to curb your behavior and adapt to the personality of your client.

In sales, research has indicated over and over again that people buy from people they like. And many people tend to like people like themselves. The sales person who portrays a chameleonlike disposition tends to have the greatest advantage and success. The key is to maintain sincerity while altering your style.

There are hundreds of personality profiles available on this subject. They are called profiles instead of tests because it is assumed that everyone has a personality; therefore there is no "pass" or "fail," as in a test. Personality profiles are valuable for sales professionals because they provide specific insights on how to "read" people.

Another value to using personality profiles is that they make you more aware of your own personality type and how your particular type works with other types.

Here is an example of a personality profile that separates personality characteristics into four quadrants: (1) Sociable, (2) Hard-Driven, (3) Devoted, and (4) Detailed. Most people fall into one of these four types. An overview of the strengths and limitations of each type follows:

Sociable	Hard-Driven
Devoted	Detailed

This profile was created to help people recognize their own key personality traits and to understand those of other people. Without this awareness, many salespeople tend to have a very myopic view of the world. With it, they find it easier to adapt to and build rapport with their prospects/customers.

The most beneficial element of this profile is that it identifies the driving force, or "hot buttons," of each personality type. For instance, what really drives the sociable personality is gaining respect, meaning recognition. (Most salespeople test sociable.) There are certain words that this type of person likes to hear, words that make him or her feel respected or recognized, like "great," "amazing," and "terrific!" The sociable personality types don't just "like" these praise phrases; they *live* for them.

Diagonally across from the sociable personality is the detailed personality. The detailed's hot button is being right. The words that compliment the detailed type are words like "You're right, absolutely, exactly, you're right again!" It's important to note that sociable-type praise phrases don't work well on detaileds. If you were to tell a detailed person that he or she is great, amazing, or terrific, that person could feel that you are being insincere. Detaileds tend to view these words as intangible and nondescript, and consequently don't get as much of a positive surge from them. As a matter of fact, many detaileds may find these words a bit nauseating. Many detaileds cannot even say sociable-type words as compliments. Instead they come out sounding sarcastic, or have an uncontrollable facial sneer.

Since the concept of "right" is such a hot button for the detailed, you had better beware when one uses the word "wrong." To a detailed personality type, *right* is *right,* and *wrong* is *wrong.*

Why are detaileds so enthralled with the concept of being right? Because most *are* right the majority of the time. They do something called "research," which sociables are less likely to do. The philosophy of the detailed is to be steady and consistent. Detaileds are procedural (like, Ready, Aim, Shoot!), whereas sociables are more random (as in Ready, Shoot, Aim!).

Detaileds are step-by-step people. Sociables fake it 'til they make it!

Communication breaks down between quadrants when one quadrant is not in tune with the language of another. For instance, the detailed gets great enjoyment out of being right. The sociable is not usually as concerned with being right; he or she would rather be amazing! So, when a detailed tells a sociable, "You're right," the sociable doesn't recognize that it is a compliment. I have a friend who is a detailed (and I'm a sociable). She tells me that I'm amazing, and I say, "You're right!" And we get along just fine.

This information on personality profiling is useful in your personal life as well. Being a sales professional, I am a sociable, and my husband (a homebuilder) is a detailed. (Occupation is a good indicator of personality type.) My husband was building an addition on our home and I was complimenting him (so I thought). I said, "Honey, the addition is so beautiful, it's just wonderful!" And he said "Yeah, yeah, yeah." Obviously I wasn't hitting his hot buttons. So I changed the compliments to be detailed by saying, "The way you aligned those beams is just perfect." That's when I got a positive response. People respond positively to the language of their type.

Let's move on to the next quadrant: the devoted personality. The hot button of the devoted is helping. Meaning that you can count on them. The devoted is a peacemaker who likes to help. The words to say to compliment a devoted personality are: "You are so devoted, so dedicated, so helpful!" Another key phrase is, "I couldn't have done it without you!" Devoteds like to help others and be included.

The fourth type is hard-driven. This type has a hot button to win. You don't have to compliment hard-driven people very much because they are already telling themselves how great they are on a daily basis. This type, if you were to offer compliments, would like to hear practical and concise information. If you can get them results that make sense, you will get their attention.

Hard-driven types like to make sense out of information. They are usually good leaders. Many have the philosophy "Help me to win, or get out of my way."

Counting through the Silence

One very important thing to be aware of is that hard-driven and detailed types think silently, and sociable and devoted types think aloud. Many sales professionals find lengthy silences intimidating. So they talk to ease their nerves. What they are actually doing is interrupting the thought process of the prospect/customer. There is a technique that works very well to control the situation. If you count silently to ten, you will realize how long the silence is, so it doesn't weigh as much on you. After the ten seconds of silence you can say, "It seems like you're giving this quite a bit of thought. Could you please share your thoughts with me?"

Of course, many people have a variety of personality traits within them. The key element to keep in mind is that each person usually has a dominant hot button in one quadrant or another. Once you detect which quadrant is the dominant one, you can drastically improve the quality of the relationship. This allows the sales professional to take customer-focused selling to a higher level.

Here are three ways to detect who is which type:

Vocabulary: People tend to use the vocabulary of their own type. If you listen carefully, you can detect it.

Occupation: Many people tend to migrate toward the profession that suits their personality type.

Body language and facial expressions: Many sociables and devoteds are more overt with their body language and facial expressions than detaileds and hard-drivens.

IMPLEMENTING INVOLVEMENT

During your sales presentation, it is crucial to get the prospect/customer involved in the conversation as soon as possible.

As was mentioned in Chapter 5, there are many methods for getting the prospect/customer involved: (1) telling stories; (2) using analogies; (3) asking questions; and (4) bringing show-and-tell items.

As you conduct the sales call it is best to use a variety of these involvement methods to gain and sustain the prospect/customer's interest.

There are two additional ways to involve your prospect/customer: "FAB" and differentiation. The acronym FAB stands for *features and benefits.* A feature is what a product or service does. A bene-

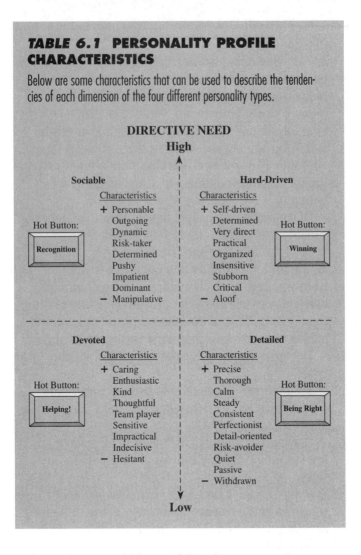

TABLE 6.1 PERSONALITY PROFILE CHARACTERISTICS

Below are some characteristics that can be used to describe the tendencies of each dimension of the four different personality types.

DIRECTIVE NEED

High

Sociable

Hot Button: **Recognition**

Characteristics
+ Personable
  Outgoing
  Dynamic
  Risk-taker
  Determined
  Pushy
  Impatient
  Dominant
− Manipulative

Hard-Driven

Hot Button: **Winning**

Characteristics
+ Self-driven
  Determined
  Very direct
  Practical
  Organized
  Insensitive
  Stubborn
  Critical
− Aloof

Devoted

Hot Button: **Helping!**

Characteristics
+ Caring
  Enthusiastic
  Kind
  Thoughtful
  Team player
  Sensitive
  Impractical
  Indecisive
− Hesitant

Detailed

Hot Button: **Being Right**

Characteristics
+ Precise
  Thorough
  Calm
  Steady
  Consistent
  Perfectionist
  Detail-oriented
  Risk-avoider
  Quiet
  Passive
− Withdrawn

Low

fit is why it would be useful to the prospect/customer. Throughout the sales call it is necessary to weave into the conversation the features and benefits of the product/service.

If we were to use a fax machine as an example, the feature would be that a fax machine can transport a document from point A to point B in fewer than 30 seconds. The benefit would be that it takes far less time than overnight mail or messenger and costs only the price of a phone call.

Another involvement technique to use during a sales call is differentiation. Differentiation entails stating what makes you different from or better than all the rest. I used to work for a company that had a list of over 30 differentiation items. The new recruits were required to memorize all 30 differentiation statements and be prepared to recite them at our weekly sales meetings. Our vice president would bring a pack of matches, and one by one each of us would have to strike a match and say as many differentiation statements as we could think of before the match flame reached our fingers. This exercise certainly created a sense of urgency. Some participants got really good at it, and were able to gain more time by licking two fingers, grabbing the half-burnt match at the top, and allowing the flame to burn down to the very bottom. Below are a few examples of differentiation points that were meaningful to our prospects and customers:

- We are a local resource.
- We have more Certified Personnel Consultants than any competitor.
- We provide one-stop shopping. We do it all and save you time and money.
- We customize to adapt to your exact need and circumstance.
- We have free 24-hour support services that answer your call before the third ring.
- You will always get a live person's voice answering the phone.
- We guarantee delivery on time every time.
- We provide a 110 percent guarantee. If you are not completely satisfied, we will provide you with a complete refund, plus an additional 10 percent.
- We do all of the detail work so that you don't have to.

A second way to involve your customer by using differentiation is to create a list of everything that makes *you* (the sales professional) different or better to work with than anyone else. For example, if you are selling pharmaceuticals and you have a nursing degree, your prospect/customer would benefit from your added professional knowledge. I once met a financial planner who bought a two-acre plot of land at the age of seventeen and built a home on it by age nineteen. This information gave me assurance that I was working with someone who knew how to set and actualize goals.

What do you have in your background that your customer needs to know about? Make a list of all your attributes and on sales calls weave them into the conversation to build the customer's confidence that you are the best person to be working with.

Why compare yourself with others? No one in the entire world can do a better job of being you than you.

Susan Carlson

No-Dumping Zone (Please!)

Once you have compiled an abundance of differentiation statements about yourself and your company, you must be careful not to go into the sales call and do a data dump. It is so tempting to tell the contact person all the great reasons why he or she should do business with you and your organization. It is much more effective, however, to wait until you uncover a specific need or concern and then mention the differentiation statements that best address that concern. It takes discipline to hold back, but the rewards are plentiful. By aligning your differentiation statements with the needs of your prospect/customer, you strengthen the bond between you, and increase the probability of a sale.

Encourage Involvement by Sharing a Piece of Yourself

One sales professional involves her prospects/customers in a different way than most. She makes a point during the sales call of mentioning something about her personal life. For example, she was going to use her vacation time to go to Nashville to record a country-and-western song. She had always had a passion for singing and decided to give it a go! She mentioned this to prospects/customers as a way of differentiating herself from all of the other sales reps out there. By sharing this information, people remembered her more and even thought of her and wanted to hear about how things went. They looked forward to reconnecting.

Another salesperson happens to mention somewhere along the line on sales calls that her daughter collects key chains. Just that brief personal comment sticks in people's minds. She has received many key chains from prospects/clients—and more business as well—by sharing a slice of her personal life with others.

IMPLEMENTING QUESTIONING

In Chapter 5 we discussed the various types of questions to ask on sales calls. In this section on the implementation process it is important to be aware of a subtle yet powerful method of questioning called the "Baldridge Bounce" (named after my family).

This concept came to my attention when I was teaching a reading and study skills program for my parents' organization, Baldridge Reading and Study Skills, Inc., of Greenwich, Connecticut.

I was teaching at a very well-to-do girls' school and was at lunch (home style) in the formal dining room, when one of my students, Suzie, asked, "Ms. Baldridge, would you care for some mashed potatoes?" I was trying to use my best etiquette (since I am not related to Leticia Baldrige) and said, "No thank you, Suzie."

Suzie then turned to her friend Patricia who was sitting next to me and asked, "Patricia, would you care for some mashed potatoes?" And Patricia said, "No thank you. But, would *you?*" And she handed Suzie the bowl of potatoes!

I was amazed by this and left the lunch wondering what had just taken place. I obviously had missed something. I went back to the office, explained to my dad what had transpired at lunch, and asked him what had really occurred. He said, "Oh, in their culture they are taught to be very altruistic. They are taught only to give, not to ask for things for themselves." I immediately responded by saying, "But they'll starve in the real world!" To which he replied, "No they won't. They have trust funds."

I still wanted to probe this whole phenomenon some more, so I said, "But this is not the real world." Upon which he replied, "Oh, but it is. Many people will ask a question when they want something, instead of blatantly expressing their desire. For example, did you go shopping with Mary last weekend?" "Yes" I replied. "Did you get hungry at some point?" "Yes." Then did you say, "I'm hungry, let's eat"? "No." "What did you say?" "Are you hungry, Mary?"

The key to this concept is realizing that people don't typically ask for what they want. They are usually far more subtle. Many times they will ask you a question, not because they want to know your views on the subject, but because they want to talk about it and share *their* views. Therefore knowing about the Baldridge Bounce technique allows you to learn much more about what's on someone's mind if you answer the question that is asked you and then bounce it back to them.

For example, Chuck, a client of mine, asked me what my thoughts were on the economy. Well, I had no idea what my thoughts were, and his question made me nervous because I didn't want to sound stupid. Have you ever been asked a question that put you on the spot? What did you do? Did you do what most salespeople do and avoid it by ever so discreetly changing the subject?

Well, I decided that in this case I would use the Baldridge Bounce technique, which is to answer the question and then bounce it back. That's exactly what I did. I said, "Chuck, I haven't really given it much thought; how do *you* feel about the economy?" And he told me how he felt. And much of the information he shared had a lot to do with the way we would be doing business together in the future.

Without being aware of this technique, I would have probably changed the subject out of pure nervousness and missed an opportunity to learn and sell more effectively.

Another example of a beneficial way to use the Baldridge Bounce was an incident on the golf course. One of my clients is a publisher. He admits to having a big ego and loves to talk about the success of his publication. He attended a seminar I conducted advocating the use of the Baldridge Bounce. The next day he was on the golf course with a client and the client asked, "How's business?" Usually, the publisher would have gone on and on about how great business was, but instead, he said, "Business is great. And I'm going to tell you all about it, over lunch. But I'm curious, how's business going for you?" Upon which the client started to go into detail about how business was going. The publisher listened intently, and after the game he positioned his presentation around the information he had obtained by bouncing back the question he was asked. He told me that it worked brilliantly.

Another benefit to using the Baldridge Bounce is that it makes people feel important. It shows that you care about the other person and that you are considerate and thoughtful.

I recently missed a bounced opportunity when my friend Mark and I were having lunch. He asked if I had gotten a vanity license plate for my new Jeep. I said, "No." When I walked him to his car, he had a vanity plate on it! It said "Balance" N.J. It was a good thing that I hadn't said, "No, because I think they're really stupid!" (Even though I don't.) Just think about how many times you may have put your foot in your mouth without even realizing it! Of course, what I could have said was, "I don't have one, but do you?" (The Baldridge Bounce). This would have led him to talk about vanity license plates, something that seemed to be important to him.

By using the bounce-back technique, you will find out more about your prospects/customers and reduce your chances of offending them, while increasing your chances of gaining useful knowledge.

BOTTOM LINE **Learn More with the Baldridge Bounce**
People usually ask questions about topics they want to talk about. Use the bounce-back to learn.

 IMPLEMENTING LISTENING SKILLS
As was mentioned in Chapter 5, listening is a crucial part of the sales process. Since we know that interference causes forgetting, there are some highly effective ways to become a better listener.

Jot-a-Thought®

One memory enhancing method is called "Jot-a-Thought."® It is a good technique to use when a thought pops into your mind and diverts your attention. What you do is have a notepad handy during sales calls, and while you are taking notes on the conversation, keep the right margin free to jot any random thoughts as they pop into your head. Once they are written down, you no longer have to think of them. They are captured on paper, to be dealt with later. So you can refocus your attention on the conversation.

Remembering Names and Facts

Another obstacle that salespeople face regarding listening is remembering names and key facts. Interference causes forgetting, and there is so much interference that occurs during the day. But there is a method to help in remembering names and facts. Follow these three simple steps.

- *Step 1.* "Say it five times and it's yours." If you repeat the name five times aloud or silently to yourself, you will increase the chances of retaining it.

- *Step 2.* Visualize it. If you write the name in your mind, making a mental picture of it, you will imprint it.

- *Step 3.* Associate it. Make an association. Link this name with something that would remind you of it.

By following these three steps you will find yourself listening more actively and remembering more too.

Closing the Communication Loop

You can assure effective communications between yourself and the prospect/client by taking 100 percent responsibility for it. Many sales professionals believe that clear communication is a 50/50 responsibility. This is not true. The sales professional needs to expect to be 100 percent responsible for the communication to be completely understood.

Many think that effective communication is demonstrated in the analogy of a pitcher throwing a ball to a catcher. Once the catcher catches the ball, the message has been received. But experts like to take the process further. After the catcher has caught the ball and then thrown it back to the pitcher is when the process is really complete.

The Mirror Method and Check®

The mirror method and check® is a technique that ensures that the communication process is working. This method entails repeating back a statement you heard, to verify that the message was correctly understood, and then asking a checking (or verifying) question as a final confirmation.

I can vividly recall the first time I employed this technique. I was visiting a prospect, and toward the end of our meeting I applied the mirror method and check technique by saying, "So, basically what you are looking for is this, this, and this. (Mirror method.) Is that right?" (Check.)

I'll never forget the look on the prospect's face. He said, "That's right! That's exactly it!" The enthusiasm in his voice conveyed the excitement that I completely understood what he wanted. I felt good about applying the technique because it was obviously working. He acted as though I was the only one who had actually heard what he had to say that day.

One hour later, I had another sales call. I was eager to use the mirror method again. As soon as I had the first opportunity, I said, "So, what you are looking for is this, this, and this." (Mirror.) "Is that right?" (Checking.) Well, he looked at me with an annoyed stare, and clenched his fist and banged it on his desk as he exclaimed, "No! That's not what I want at all!" "Uh-oh," I thought. "Now what do I do?" I had repeated exactly what he had just said he wanted. I couldn't believe what was happening to me. Luckily I remembered a customer service technique: "When in doubt, blame yourself." So I said, "I'm sorry, I must have misunderstood what you said. What is it that you're looking for?" (I didn't say what I really wanted to, which was, "Hey, I just repeated everything you said back to you; what do you mean that's not it?!") The prospect went on to say, "I need this, this, and this." After which I confirmed what he said and eagerly ended the meeting.

When reviewing the two back-to-back sales calls in my mind, I couldn't believe how using the same technique could produce two completely opposite responses. Because the latter call had rattled me so, I was seriously contemplating abandoning it. But then I realized that it had worked equally as well as the former call in clarifying the communication. If I had not mirrored and checked, I would have wasted time drafting a proposal that was not what the prospect had wanted. So, despite the uncomfortable confrontation, I was very clear about the thoughts the prospect had intended to convey.

After giving more thought to what had happened on that second sales call I came to the conclusion that the reason why the prospect vehemently disagreed with the mirror and check regarding what he said, was because when I used the technique he heard what he had said and disagreed with himself! Then, he thought more about what he wanted and switched to a better idea. I just acted as a sounding board reflecting the thoughts back to him.

So, it is necessary to expect an array of reactions when applying this technique. Whatever the response, you can expect to have a better understanding of your prospect/client's needs by using the process.

DANGER! ## Avoid Being a Parrot

When using the mirror method be careful not to repeat verbatim what the client is saying in a monotone voice tone, or he or she may annoyingly reply, "That's what I just said!" Instead, say a phrase like, "to summarize," "to clarify," "to verify," "to review." These phrases act as sophisticated transitional phrases. Then paraphrase the meaning of what you believe he/she is saying.

ACTIVE VERSUS PASSIVE LISTENING

On sales calls, active listening is essential. Active listening involves "attending" to the message sent and understanding the content as well as the intent. There is actually a listening institute in St. Louis, Missouri, that has several definitions for the verb "to listen." One of my favorites is that the word "listen" comes from two Anglo-Saxon words that mean to hear and to wait in suspense. Can you imagine listening so intently that you are waiting in suspense for each word to come out of the speaker's mouth?

The staff at the Listening Institute studied the body language of a person listening intently and compared it to the body language of a person watching a cliff-hanger movie. The similarities were astounding. Both were leaning forward, with eyes widened. This is the opposite of how passive listeners act. In passive listening the listener is not completely focusing on the message and allows distractions and interruptions to consume him or her.

Active listeners get more sales because they are better able to understand the specific needs of the prospect/customer. Attentive listeners are more likely to come up with creative and practical solutions for using their prospect/customer's product or service.

KEY CONCEPT — IMPLEMENTING THE SATISFACTION CONTINUUM

During the sales call the most effective way to utilize the satisfaction continuum is to keep it in mind. If you are continually thinking about what needs to be said in this meeting to gain the prospect's/client's highest level of satisfaction without sacrificing your own satisfaction level, that's the first step.

To achieve this it is necessary to ask a series of checking questions to confirm your perception of the prospect's/client's satisfaction level. What you may think is important to the client may actually be of less value to him or her. (Examples of checking questions appear in Chapter 5.)

Two stories are classic examples of the importance of being aware of perceived value. The first tells of a father and his two daughters. The daughters were fighting over an orange. Finally, to settle the argument the father said they would have to split it. The daughters thought that a fair solution, so one girl cut the orange in half and the other selected which half she wanted. Both seemed equally satisfied.

The fascinating part of the story is what occurred afterward. The father was surprised to discover that one of the girls ate the orange and threw away the peel, while the other girl used the peel for cooking and threw away the orange. Could there have been a better deal here? Of course the outcome could have been doubly satisfying if checking questions had been used to learn the users' needs and intentions.

The second story is about a boy named Jimmy who was selling a puppy. He put a sign in front of his house that read: "Puppy for Sale." A man was driving past the house with his kids when the kids screamed, "Stop the car! Can we please go see the puppy?" They had been in the market to buy a dog, so the man stopped the car and went up to the front door and said, "I might be interested in

uppy. How much do you want for her?"
ny said, "I'm asking $10,000." The man said,
0,000! You must be kidding! That dog isn't
vorth $10,000." And he drove away.

A week later the same man drove by again. He noticed that the sign was gone from in front of Jimmy's house. His curiosity got the best of him, and he just had to stop the car and ask about the puppy. He knocked at the front door, and Jimmy answered. The man said, "Hey, did you sell your puppy?" "Sure did," said Jimmy. "I bet you didn't get full price for him." "Oh, but I did," replied Jimmy. The man said, "You mean to tell me that you got $10,000 for your puppy?" "Yes, answered Jimmy. Tommy from next door came by with two $5,000 kittens and we made an even trade."

BOTTOM LINE Find Real Value

The prospect's/client's satisfaction level is a perception that the sales professional must discover by asking checking questions to determine the real value.

KEY CONCEPT OBJECTION! OBJECTION!

During a sales call it is important to uncover and handle objections in order to effectively advance the sale. Many sales professionals are relieved to end a sales call without receiving any objections. They assume that the client is interested. But more often than not, this is an incorrect assumption. When things are going smoothly on a sales call many sales professionals are afraid to "rock the boat" and therefore avoid initiating any discussion that might lead to objections. Yet, smoking out objections helps you to determine the interest level of the prospect/customer.

To uncover objections during a sales call, ask probing questions like these:

- "Based on this conversation, what do you like about what you've seen? And, on the other hand, what concerns might you have?"
- "Who else have you been meeting with?"
- "Who else are you considering working with?"
- "What kind of budget do you have for this?"

- "How do you envision working with us?"
- "Who is your top choice right now?"
- "When do you expect to know your final decision?"
- "Can you describe the decision-making process, including the steps and people involved, please?"

I recall reading about the concept of embracing objections when I was first starting out in sales some years ago. I just couldn't buy into it. It seemed too scary. But finally I decided to give it a try on a sales call. I asked the probing question, "What would prevent you from using me as your keynote speaker at the meeting?" The prospect said flatly, "If Jane Conley is available." I asked, "Why is that?" (Chaser question.) She replied bluntly, "In addition to her 20 years of experience in our industry, she was recommended strongly by one of our major clients."

I was contemplating saying as a comeback, "Some people select me as their speaker over industry experts to get a different perspective." But my gut feeling was not to go that route. My next question was, "Then why did you meet with me today if you have decided on the speaker? (Were those words coming out of *my* mouth?!) She replied, "Naturally, in case she is unavailable. The meeting will be on a Saturday in June, and I am not sure if she is willing to work on weekends. Do you work weekends?" "Yes," I replied. "Are you free on the 11th?" "Yes." I could see that she was impatient and ready to end this meeting abruptly, so I asked, "When should I follow-up?" She said, "I will know by noon tomorrow." I told her I would call her the next day. As I left that sales call I felt a little uncomfortable—probably because it was the first time I was asking questions that I was afraid to know the answers to.

As I had expected, Jane Conley got the speaking engagement. Yet, I didn't feel as disappointed as I thought I would. It was because I knew where I stood when I made the call. I find that so many sales professionals go on sales calls, have a nice chat, leave without getting an objection, and hope that they will get the business. Then they get discouraged when they don't. By using the sample

...t of probing questions on the previous page on ...les calls, you will be able to uncover objections and deal with them.

 Objection Handling

On sales calls, objections need to be acknowledged and handled appropriately. There are many techniques to handle objections on sales calls; these include the following:

- Repeat the objection to make sure that you clearly understand it, and that the prospect/client agrees that it is correct.

- Isolate the objection by asking, "Is that the main reason of concern or are there any other reasons?"

- Seek a commitment by isolating the objective further, by asking, "If we can alleviate this concern, would you be able to commit to working with us?"

- Ask if the price is a key factor. Many prospects/customers are hesitant to discuss price concerns because they are uncertain whether there is flexibility, and they may not want to be offensive.

- Go for the close. Ask for the next step.

- Offer to be a backup vendor if someone else is selected. Backups move forward rapidly when problems occur with current vendors—and problems do occur.

One of the most widely and successfully used objection-handling techniques is called "Feel, Felt, Found." When you encounter an objection, say the following: "I understand how you feel. As a matter of fact many of my best customers initially felt the same way. What they found was . . ." This technique is very effective because it allows you to empathize with the prospects/customers. You are not only agreeing that you may not be right for them, you are also letting them know that they are not alone—that other people have felt the same way. Then you make a U-turn by saying, "And what they found is . . ." Which conveys that despite the initial concern, it was worthwhile to meet after all.

The Feel, Felt, Found technique needs to be followed by a closing statement such as, "So, when can we meet?"

BEWARE THE RAPID AND CANNED COMEBACK

The Feel, Felt, Found technique is one that is widely known in the sales field, as well as in business. So it is important to be careful not to respond with this comeback too quickly or in too rehearsed a manner, or you will be perceived as being canned and insincere. Therefore you should avoid using the exact model stated above. Interject different but similar words into the model to gain the same results in a more discreet fashion. Here are a few other ways to say the Feel, Felt, Found technique:

Instead of saying, "I understand how you feel," use one of the following statements:

- "I understand your concern."
- "I hear what you're saying."
- "I realize this may not be the best time."

Next, instead of "Many of my best customers initially felt the same way," say:

- "Many of my best customers initially had the same concerns."
- "It is a common concern that I've heard expressed many times."
- "Many of my best customers initially expressed the same concerns."
- "Many thought the same thing."

And exchange the statement, "What they found was . . ." with one of the following:

- "What they discovered was . . ."
- "What they learned was . . ."
- "What they realized was . . ."
- "What they came to find out was . . ."

Also, be careful to avoid using the word "but" as a transition, because it can act as an eraser and wipe out the positive verbal foundation you have created.

NEXT-STEP SELLING

Next-step selling is closing. The term "next-step selling" is being used here because in es the "close" at the end of a sales call is close of the sale. It is, more often, the e next step in the sales process. Since it kes five to seven "next-step" closes to close an actual sale, it is essential that you have available a wide assortment of closing techniques for use throughout the entire sales process.

This section will cover several highly effective closing strategies. It is important, when analyzing the elements of a sales cycle, to remember that closing is a process—meaning that the close is really a series of mini-closes that are done throughout the entire sales interaction. The close actually begins when the first contact is made. As a matter of fact, if you set up the relationship properly from the very beginning, you will find the prospect/customer closing *you* at the end. (I love it when that happens!)

FIVE SUREFIRE WAYS TO CLOSE THE SALE
The Multiple Close

The multiple close entails providing the prospect/customer with choices and options. Most people like to have options, and they like to make comparisons. Therefore, it is usually best to go into the final sales call with more than one solution. This is important for many reasons, including the following:

1. When the prospect/customer asks, after you give your best pitch, "What else do you have?" you will have something to say beside "Gulp!"

2. If you are competing against another organization for the business, it gives you strength in numbers. The prospect can choose between "them" or you, and you or you. (Three options are usually the best number to provide.)

3. There are usually three types of buyers. To use a car analogy, one type would be the top-of-the-line luxury buyer, the one who favors a Mercedes or Lexus. Then there's the middle-of-the-road type buyer, the Taurus, Grand Am type. And finally, the low budget no-frills buyer, such as the Hyundai, Kia type. By providing three choices during your sales call, you will be providing something for everybody. And in doing so, you will increase your probability of success.

3 types of buyers

140

The Pain and Pleasure Principle

Some sales professionals hesitate in using the pain and pleasure principle because they feel it may be perceived as a negative way to sell. Why don't you be the judge of that?

The pain and pleasure principle entails finding your prospect's/customer's pain (their obstacle), making it hurt (recognizing it as a major barrier), and then making it better (providing a solution) through your product or service.

focus on their problem + then solve it for them

Here are four examples of the pain and pleasure principle in sales that work brilliantly:

The first is the classic headache commercial on television. When the commercial begins, you see a close-up of someone's face, which appears to be in tremendous pain. Then you hear screaming children in the background, and the face scrunches up to show even more pain. Next, you see a bottle of aspirin. The person takes two, and as the commercial ends, the birds are chirping, the sun is shining brightly, and a wide smile appears on the person's face.

The next two examples both have to do with the car repair industry. Generally these commercials are heard on the radio—usually while you are in the car on your way to or from work. In one the announcer says, "Do you feel your transmission slipping? You know how that feels; you press your foot on the gas, and the engine just doesn't feel like it is as powerful as it could be. You may need a new transmission. Why not come in for a free evaluation. No obligation. Just call . . . to make an appointment with our expert technicians. You'll be glad you did."

And what happens when you hear this? I don't know about you, but it makes me feel like my transmission is slipping. I start to wonder whether I should check it out. The same uncertainty occurs with muffler commercials on the car radio. As soon as you hear the commercial, your muffler starts to sound louder. Must be the power of suggestion. It also has to do with the FUD factor. FUD is an acronym for "Fear, Uncertainty, and Doubt." The philosophy is that if you can make the prospect/customer aware of the foreseeable, and even the unforeseeable, obstacles that are out there, it allows you to troubleshoot probable solutions and prevent problems from occurring. You can take the role of a consultant working toward creating practical solutions by using your product/service.

The fourth example is when the vacuum cleaner salesperson "comes a calling." When I was a recruiter of sales professionals, I interviewed one. He told me that he sold five vacuum cleaners a week. Which is a lot, considering that he was calling on people who were rarely ever home, and considering that each vacuum cleaner sold for approximately $1,200!

I was curious how he was able to sell so many, so I asked him. He said that he was able to get in the door by saying that his company was running a contest to win a trip to Disney World for his family; all he had to do was demonstrate the vacuum cleaner. (I was familiar with this approach because the guy who sold me mine just happened to use it, too!)

"But how do you close the sale?" I asked. "Well," he replied, "once I get them in the bedroom, I really score!" I said, "Excuse me!?" He said, "Oh, I'm sorry, I didn't mean it like that. I just mean that the bedroom is where the real dirt is." "What exactly do you do in the bedroom?" I hesitantly asked. "I vacuum the bed, of course," he said, "because that is where the dirt is. You see, most people don't realize how much dust and dirt accumulates in their beds. I simply show them, by vacuuming the beds in the house. Then I make the connection that the dust and dirt they have been unaware of may be linked to allergies.

"When I ask if anyone in the house has allergies, the majority of the time somebody does—do you know anyone who doesn't have allergies these days? Then I ask about the allergist visits, the shots, and the bills, to increase the necessity to buy. Another obvious connection can be made between the dust and dirt and any headaches they may be experiencing. The solution, of course, is in making an investment in controlling the particles in the environment and thus improving their family's health and well-being by purchasing my product. It works just about every time."

This method made sense. In order to close the sale, this sales rep was using the pain and pleasure principle to perfection, and it was working for him. Now this might seem too manipulative for you, or negative or unprofessional, but when used correctly it gets results. And it does so without being manipulative at all. The key is to use it correctly. How? The best way is to brainstorm all the possible obstacles that your prospect/customer may encounter by not using your product/service, or by using your competition's product/service instead of yours. Then toss the ideas that don't seem viable, and expand on those that do. Now you are taking the role of a professional consultant versus a charlatan, or the voice of gloom and doom.

The Puppy Dog Close

Although the "puppy dog" close was created ages ago, it is still highly effective today. The story behind the unusual name of this close goes like this:

A pet storeowner sees a family eyeing a cute puppy in a cage in his shop. He takes the puppy out of the cage and places it in the hands of one of the family members. The puppy is happily wagging its tale and licking the person holding it. The storeowner says, "He likes you! Why don't you take him home for a few days?" Once the puppy goes home he usually does not come back to the store. This technique is also referred to as the trial close. It is used in any industry from copiers to computers. Once a copier, for example, is placed in the copier room of an organization, no one seems to want to use the old one. In comparison it's simply not as good as the new one being tried out. The sale is inevitable. Computer software is also sold many times in a trial close. The philosophy is, in effect, to "just take it with you with no obligation. If you find it is better than what you are currently using, keep it and we'll just bill you."

*[handwritten margin note: * trial close — why don't you try it for a few days?]*

The Benjamin Franklin Close

[handwritten margin note: weigh the pros + cons + then decide]

The Benjamin Franklin close supposedly originated from a story about how Benjamin Franklin made decisions. It was said that he would compile pro and con lists and then weigh his options. The way to use this concept effectively on a sales call is to go over all the deciding factors related to the purchase and make these facts tangible by writing them down. The process of doing this exercise allows for clarity, then acts as a sounding board for your prospect/customer. This will allow him or her to think through the advantages versus the disadvantages, and come to a sound decision. If you gain the trust of your prospects/customers, you will be included in this decision-making process. If you don't gain their trust, you will be excluded.

The Alternative Choice Close

The alternative choice close entails offering your prospect/customer an "either/or" solution. The way it is used is by asking closed-ended questions like, "Would you like to meet again on Tuesday or on Thursday?" "Are you free in the morning or in the afternoon?" The alternative choice close allows for the sales executive to pinpoint a commitment by suggesting an alternative. This close is usually used to get the prospect/customer to make simple decisions quickly. The drawback to this close is that it can seem pushy or obnoxious if it is overused.

Reminder: The close in a word is: "When?" . . . "When can we meet?" . . . "When can you authorize?" . . . "When can I follow-up with you?" . . . "When can we deliver?"

BOTTOM LINE **ALWAYS BE CLOSING**

It is critical to use your ABCs when selling. Always Be Closing!

CONDUCT SALES CALLS THAT GET RESULTS

Results-driven sales calls require a tremendous amount of thought and organization.

There are eight main steps to conducting sales calls that get results. First, create the structure or foundation of the meeting. Next, focus on the customer more than on yourself, and use techniques such as stories, questions, analogies, and show-and-tell props to build rapport and sustain interest.

Keep in mind that listening is a skill, and that you need to be actively tuned in to the customer and warding off distractions, both internal and external, that interfere with the listening process.

The ultimate goal of your sales call is to discover how to satisfy the customer's needs as you satisfy your own. This involves finding objections by asking the right probing questions. And finally, once all uncovered objections are revealed and dealt with, it's time to close with a puppy dog, Benjamin Franklin, or pain-and-pleasure statement that lead you and the customer to the ultimate closing question: "When?"

The Best Technology for Successful Selling

Never tell your computer that you're in a hurry.

anonymous

Technology has come to play a critical role in achieving self-managed sales success. And today more technology is available for sales professionals than ever before. In fact, with new options entering the market on an almost daily basis, it seems virtually impossible to keep up with current and future trends. Technology in all fields is definitely in a fast-forward mode, with no sign of slowing down.

Some sales professionals (but not nearly enough of them) comfortably embrace change. They discover and rapidly implement new systems that they find to be helpful. Others, who are resistant to change, are still trying to adapt to being thrown into the computer age. They are struggling to learn how to take advantage of the World Wide Web and all its riches.

There are many multimillion-dollar sales producers who don't even know how to turn on a computer. On the other hand, there are many who could never generate their top-level revenue *without* their computer. Whether you love technology, or loathe it, it is here to stay.

This chapter will explore a wide range of technological devices, and provide insight into the pros and cons of using them. Please keep in mind, however, that it has been written by a *sales* expert, not a technology expert. It is not intended to be a comprehensive catalogue of every type of technology, but it will provide sales professionals with the basic information they need regarding industry-specific technology tools. Many of the items listed are necessities, while others may be considered luxuries. (The interesting thing is that in one to two years from the copyright date of this book, some of today's luxuries will have become necessities, which reminds me of a quote that I once heard: "The difference between a luxury and a necessity is price.")

TELEPHONE

The telephone is still the tried and true mechanism that sales professionals rely on to initiate contact with potential and existing customers. There are an enormous number of features that have modified the basic telephone during recent years. Here is a list of some telephone essentials:

Speed-Dial

Speed-dial allows you to program your telephone to store up to x number of telephone numbers. Once it is programmed correctly, you can press a one- or two-digit number to dial the telephone number instead of the standard seven to eight digits. Cumulatively speaking, this can save an enormous amount of time. It is usually best to store the most frequently called telephone numbers first, and then work your way down the list. The downside to speed-dial is that if you are calling from any phone other than your own, you may not recall the full number because you are so used to speed-dialing it. On a personal note, I have actually called people who didn't even know the work phone number for their spouse because they had come to rely so heavily on speed-dial.

Use Speed-Dial for Call Planning

One creative way to use speed-dial that I learned from sales expert Mark S. A. Smith, coauthor of *Guerrilla Negotiating,* part of the *Guerrilla Sales* book series, is to plan cold calls the night before and program the first two calls on your call list into speed-dial. This way, in the morning, you can get into action quickly, without procrastination or disorganization.

Voice Mail

The curious thing about voice mail is that when it first came out, no one would talk on it. Now, you can't get anyone to *stop* talking on it.

The advantages of voice mail outweigh the disadvantages. Some of the advantages are as follows:

- Quick way to leave a message.
- Quick way to communicate information.
- Twenty-four-hour accessibility.
- Outbound message capabilities: Lets people know where you are and what you are doing.
- Gives you a second chance to make a good first impression. If you can "crack the code" by hitting 1 or # after leaving your message, you may have a chance to review and to change it. Unfortunately, every system is different, so there are no guarantees.

Some of the disadvantages of voice mail are as follows:

- People talk way too long without getting to the point.
- Systems malfunction (e. g., messages get cut off or erased).
- Endless telephone tag.
- Impersonal.
- No one is there to respond or give feedback.
- No second chance to make a first impression unless you "crack the code."

The next time you get frustrated when you have to leave the umpteenth voice mail message on a client's/prospect's system, keep in mind that voice mail really is a valuable tool, and make a commitment to use it effectively. (For more on voice mail tips turn to Chapter 4.)

Caller ID

As mentioned in Chapter 3, Caller ID can be used as an excellent time management tool to control unwanted interruptions. Another benefit is that it allows you to plan before taking a call and prevents you from getting blindsided. But the downsides of Caller ID are plentiful. It used to be that when you made a mistake on a telephone call you could simply hang up and remain anonymous. Now that option is becoming less viable. Second, many callers activate a Caller ID block by pressing *xx, which disables your system. Moreover, when others become aware that you have Caller ID they may suspect (and in some cases, rightly so) that you are using it to avoid them.

Telephone Calling Cards

A calling card is a handy item for making long-distance calls while on the road. It's beneficial because when making phone calls from a pay phone, even local calls, many times it prevents the unwanted intrusion from an operator interrupting your call to request that you insert additional coins.

However, the rapid progression of digital and cellular telephones is making the calling card obsolete. It is far more convenient to be able to make calls from virtually any location, at any time, and for one flat rate, without the hassle of being literally "tied" to a pay phone. And it actually costs less.

The greatest disadvantage in using calling cards is that your calling card number can get hijacked in various ways. Some shysters will place a mechanism in or around a public telephone that records and stores the calling card number. Other scam artists will stand behind the caller as he or she is dialing a number. And others even have the audacity to use binoculars, from hidden locations, to observe a number being dialed. (Are you getting the impression that I may have been a victim of these ploys?) Why do I always feel like the only one who goes through this aggravation? Actually, it is kind of exciting, and at the same time traumatizing, to receive a $4,000 telephone bill for calls you never placed! And for calls to so many exotic places—Morocco, Argentina, Taiwan, New Zealand.

Beepers/Pagers

It seems like everyone has a beeper or a pager these days. These communication devices helped define the "24/7" workweek. I especially like the vibrate mode. Who would have ever dreamed that in a business meeting, top executives would be uttering the phrase, "Please switch to vibrate mode before we begin."

Cellular Phone

The danger of using a cellular phone is that, unlike a digital phone, thieves can rather easily gain access to your cell phone number. Without fail, when I venture into a major city (especially New York City), and use a cellular phone, upon returning to the office I get a call from my service provider questioning my call usage—followed several weeks later by a huge fraudulent telephone bill. Fortunately, there are now pin codes that can protect these thefts from occurring. The only downside is that you become obligated to dial more numbers than you may really want to.

Digital Phone

The feedback I've received from many sales professionals is that once you get past the growing pains of its newness, the digital phone is wonderful. (Isn't that the case with most technology?) I encountered an example of this several months before I finally broke down and bought my own digital phone. (I'm definitely not one of those first-kid-on-the-block-to-have-it people!) I was talking to a friend who kept raving about her digital phone. Yet, every time she called me on it, she seemed to be cursing at it (the phone, not me, I think). She would say, "You really should upgrade to a digital (pause) oh darn, I hate this thing! (pause) . . . I mean it really is the way to go (pause) . . . Oh no, not again (pause) . . . Do you want me to hook you up with my vendor? Ugh! I can't believe it, the reception is getting static-y, I'll have to call you back later." When we finally reconnected, I asked, "Why do you keep raving about this phone when every time you call me on it you sound like you hate it?" "You just have to get used to it," she said. "It's really worth all the initial aggravation."

Beware of Blackout Zones

A "blackout zone" is an area within which your service provider is unauthorized to transmit its telecommunication services. When choosing your cellular service provider, it's critically important that you inquire about blackout zones in great detail. There is a gross misconception that by just having a cellular/digital phone you will be guaranteed caller access within any area.

Many people think that a blackout zone is an area that lacks a transmission tower. This is not entirely true. Long-distance companies have been competitively gaining control over specific geographic areas, but there are definitely accessibility limitations. Being unaware of the blackout zones of your particular long-distance carrier could cost you far more than a sale—it could even endanger your life if you find yourself in an emergency situation while traveling within such a zone.

Self Caller

Believe it or not, people actually call themselves in order to interrupt long-winded telephone conversations that they'd otherwise be at the mercy of. The bottom line is that you can save time simply by using your cellular/digital phone or nearby fax phone to call yourself. Your incoming call will alert the person you're speaking with that you have another call, and that you really do have other things to do.

Teleconferencing

Teleconferencing is an excellent way to conduct a meeting without wasting valuable time traveling. It is also good to use as a follow-up tool. What makes teleconferencing work well is that the client can't actually see what you're doing during the call. So, you and your colleagues have the option to exchange written messages, if necessary, to add to the value of the conversation.

Data Conferencing

Data conferencing involves a process through a network that enables users to communicate through their computers to one another simultaneously.

Videoconferencing

In its present level of technology, videoconferencing is sort of like watching an old Godzilla movie, in that it involves a series of pauses and stiff movements, and voices that seem to be dubbed. It is in many ways efficient, however, to have face-to-face communication without the burden and expense of traveling.

Headset

Headsets are especially effective for sales professionals who prefer to stand and/or walk while speaking on the telephone. Research has shown that those who use headsets generate more call activity than those who do not. The beauty of a headset is that it enables you to speak with more expression and frees up your hands, allowing you to take notes, work the computer, and so forth.

Another advantage is that you will drastically reduce your chiropractic bills due to neck and upper back strain. But be sure to purchase the one with a quick-escape mechanism. There have been reports of people starting out with headsets for efficiency only to end up with them as a noose around their neck.

PALM PILOT

A Palm Pilot is a device that allows you to record essential business information such as names, telephone numbers, addresses, and notes regarding your prospects/customers. With this palm-sized instrument you can actually handwrite information onto a screen and it will translate your written information into typed form.

You can also load your database onto it, which allows you to have all the information you need about your prospects/clients. The downside is that the Palm Pilot only recognizes certain letters in the alphabet. Others have to be represented by special characters, which you have to memorize. There are a few models, such as one by Philips, that will allow you to use the full alphabet, yet it has it's own limitations. Many also have e-mail capabilities. A nice perk.

PORTABLE SHIATSU MASSAGER

The portable Shiatsu massager may be the answer to your uncomfortable office chair problems. This unique device can be found at The Sharper Image and other electronic specialty stores. It comes in various shapes and sizes, is usually constructed out of leather or plastic, and has two mechanical fists that jut out. These fists massage your neck and back as if they were kneading dough.

FOOT MASSAGER

Ahhhh, finally, technology that a salesperson *really* needs. Again, there are many types of foot massagers to choose from. Some are electronic and vibrate, like boards, pillows, and slippers, or others are to be used manually by rolling or walking on them. With all the walking, standing, and running that salespeople do in the course of a day, a month or a year, its definitely a good use of your time to give your feet a treat.

"You can't make footprints in the sands of time if you're sitting on your butt. And who wants to make buttprints in the sands of time?

Bob Moawad

MACINTOSH/DESKTOP COMPUTER

There has always been a battle between the advocates of the Macintosh and the PC lovers. More often than not, you either use just one or the other.

Computers in the future may weigh no more than 1.5 tons.
Popular Mechanics (1949), forecasting the relentless march of science

Laptop Computer

The laptop computer is a godsend, especially for sales professionals who are constantly on the go. The advantages are many, and include quick and accurate access to database records while on the road, and portable e-mail and fax capabilities. The laptop gives you immediate access to a word processor for typing correspondence quickly, and has download capabilities that enable you to send critical information to a satellite office from a remote location. (Always pack extra batteries and battery chargers.)

I think there is a world market for maybe five computers.
Thomas Watson, Chairman of IBM (1943)

ACT Software

The premise behind ACT software is to help the sales professional keep track of leads and contacts. It works well and is one of the most popular contact management software packages available today. ACT is frequently upgraded to keep up with the constant increases in information needed by salespeople in order to do their job. Over the years, the requirements have evolved from just having a business telephone/fax number to adding beeper/pager numbers, cellular/digital phone numbers, home numbers, e-mail addresses, web sites, even secretaries' names and numbers. And the software does an exceptional job of sorting for mailings, broadcast e-mails, and so forth.

Telemagic

This software is designed to assist telemarketing sales representatives in organizing their databases and for cueing up calls.

Gold Mine

Gold Mine is a strategic management software that helps salespeople plan and forecast. Many sales managers like this system because of these capabilities:

Additional software packages that sales professionals view as useful tools of the trade are as follows:

- Microsoft Access
- Lexis-Nexis
- Lotus Notes

PRESENTATION TECHNOLOGY

To a sales professional, presentation is everything. It has an enormous impact on the outcome of a sale. In addition to the essentials (company brochures, samples, premium gifts and business cards), below is a list of equipment that can enhance your presentation:

Microsoft PowerPoint

Microsoft PowerPoint is a software package that comes standard in Microsoft Office and can also be purchased individually. Using Microsoft Power-Point will make your audience feel that you are up on the latest technology, and gives your presentations polish. Those who use it love it because PowerPoint slides are so easy to create and the assortment of colors and graphics is so vast that the presentation really comes to life.

One of the biggest detriments to PowerPoint (and any other fancy electronic form of presentation equipment or technology) is the possibility that the technology will override the message the sales professional is seeking to convey. This is a common reality that is very important to keep in mind. Also, to avoid catastrophe, remember to charge batteries and note any product you may need to make PowerPoint work, such as an LCD projector or a TV monitor.

Overhead Projector

The overhead projector is beginning to be viewed as the dinosaur of presentation equipment. Microsoft PowerPoint is the preferred way to go due to its greater sophistication. If you do choose to use an overhead projector, it is important to create *color* transparencies; write concise information; and to include no more than three to five points per overhead, no more than three to five words per point, and to use at least a 30-point font size. (These guidelines apply when creating PowerPoint slides as well.)

It is also very important to make photocopies of the overheads to present to the prospects/customers. The same technology glitches that apply to any form of media also apply here, so plan ahead by bringing an extra light bulb and having a backup machine available.

Slide Projector

Slide projectors are great for livening up a presentation. Pictures speak a thousand words and draw people in. The downside to slide projectors is that they are subject to the same technical difficulties mentioned earlier. Also, the fact that the room needs to be darkened is a possible attention detractor. This is a point that needs to be kept in mind when using PowerPoint and overheads as well.

Laser Pointer

A laser pointer is usually a small pen-shaped object that shines an intensely focused red light on the subject it's being pointed toward. Laser pointers add a bit of sophistication to a presentation, because most people are ill-equipped when giving presentations and just use their hand or a stick pointer. When doing this, the words from the screen can end up on your arm or body, looking ridiculous. The laser pointer takes your technology level up a notch because many people think laser pointers are cool. (One danger to having a laser pointer at your meeting is if it gets into the wrong hands. You know those cruel souls who discreetly point it at the forehead of the person presenting. Just be aware that this is done—and see to it that it doesn't happen to you.)

Video

Videotapes are excellent sales visual tools that get people involved. The downside is that they need to be of an appropriate length and include subject matter that will maintain the prospect's/client's attention. Also, some videotapes need adapters because they vary in size. Once again, technical difficulties can occur—so it is important to test out the equipment before anyone arrives at your meeting. (This concept goes for all presentation equipment.)

VCR/TV Monitor

This equipment enables you to play videos and also view PowerPoint presentations. Most models (but not all) seem to work best by turning the TV to Channel 3 and then hitting the play button on the VCR. Some have remote control options; others don't. It works best if you can designate a technology person to help you by manning the VCR/TV monitor upon your cue. This makes the presentation go more smoothly and allows for the technology to flow along with it.

Digital Camera

The digital camera is a camera that is capable of taking pictures that can be downloaded and processed into a computer. It's an excellent vehicle from which to further customize any documents or correspondence, because you can take a picture of your client or yourself to add to your marketing materials or to download into your computer to e-mail.

Digital Video

Like the digital camera, digital video can run on a computer, which allows for movement to be added to your visual design capabilities.

AUTOMATED MAIL MACHINE AND SCALE

The automated mail machine is an effective piece of business technology. It makes all outgoing mail look professional and official because it has a crisp red stamp and date on it. Some models can be programmed to print a slogan along with the stamp. Using the scale saves money and avoids delivery delays; you won't overpay or underpay in postage. Also, it's important to type the addresses of outgoing correspondence. Many are handwritten and far less professional.

FAX MACHINE

Using a fax is an efficient way to keep in touch and demonstrate a sense of urgency. The nicest things about sending a fax are that it saves the prospect/client time that would have been spent opening mail and it gets your communication to him or her in a more visible and faster manner.

There are software programs (such as WinFax) that enable you to fax directly from your PC, which is a real timesaver. However, it is important to take time to proof your documents before utilizing the expediency of this system. Also, despite the availability of this great software package, very few companies that employ sales professionals have embraced it to date and therefore it is more often found in home-based offices than in corporate America.

INTERNET

The Internet is a great way to research prospects for call lists and to get background information on prospects and clients. With this technology so readily available, it is inexcusable to make a call without researching the company first.

INTRANET

The Intranet is similar to the Internet except that it is a network that exists within an organization.

WEB SITE

A web site is a vehicle that companies use to describe and promote their services to Internet users. It allows them to advertise all of the compelling reasons why a prospect/customer should work with them and their organization. It also enables a company to reach a wider audience. In addition, a web site can be linked to e-mail for quick response to inquiries. When designing web sites be careful not to include any privileged information that can be used to advantage by competitors.

Sales is a people profession. If a picture/headshot of yourself can be displayed somewhere in the site, you can have prospects and clients actually see you. It is a big benefit.

INFOTRACK

Infotrack is an on-line service that can locate virtually any article written about anyone. It is an excellent resource to use prior to going on sales calls to get a better understanding of who you are meeting with. Most library branches have Infotrack available.

SCANNER

A scanner is a handy device that saves you time by scanning business cards or documents into your computer. Scanners are available that print in both black-and-white and color. Although they are not perfect at duplicating and transcribing your document, in most cases they are still great time-savers.

CARDSCAN

CardScan is a high-performance business-card-scanning software. It allows you to scan business cards into your PC. In the sales profession, business cards are used as an essential way to conduct business. CardScan works as an information manager that keeps your contacts organized and easily retrievable. It is Palm-Pilot-compatible and offers a free upgrade. See http://www.cardscan.com for details. CardScan easily transfers data into ACT or you favorite contact manager. The one disadvantage is if your scanner is not of the highest quality, it will take more time to scan the card than to input it manually. Not only does the scanning process seem lengthy, but once the card is scanned, it requires proofing and editing. Be prepared and allow time to make these adjustments.

MICROSOFT WORD

Microsoft Word equips you with everything you need to write and create professional-looking documents and to share information both on the printed page and on the Internet. It is a powerful tool and one of the most popular word processing software packages. It also comes with Microsoft Office as an ancillary item. It is important to update your software.

If you are still using an outdated Microsoft Word program and it works for you, keep it—but the problem most sales professionals have found is that e-mail attachments from those who have not upgraded the attachments arrive in hieroglyphics that are impossible to read.

640K ought to be enough for anybody.
Bill Gates (1981)

E-MAIL

E-mail has really taken off. Some people no longer use voicemail, because they find e-mail so much more efficient (see an example of this in Chapter 4). The benefits of e-mail are great; for example, you can get your message in front of someone without being blocked by a receptionist or secretary, and e-mail is a quick and cost-effective way to connect and keep in touch because information is easy to send and receive.

I witnessed an interaction at a trade show a few years ago, where two people were exchanging business cards in a tradeshow booth. (For tips on how to work a tradeshow, turn to Chapter 4.) The prospect was extremely interested in the product the salesperson was selling, and said to him, "I'd like to learn more about how we might be able to work together. Let's keep in touch. What's your e-mail address? I don't see it on your card." The salesperson responded that he didn't have one. The prospect shook his head in disbelief and said

"Oh, forget it!" and walked away. The moral of the story: E-mail is an essential business tool. If you don't have it, get it. Once you get it, use it. Just be sure to use it with those who like it, and stick to phone, voice mail, and fax with those who prefer those methods of communication. It is up to you to ask which mode of communication best suits your prospect/customer, and then to comply.

The downside to e-mail is that no one gets to hear your voice, and you don't get to hear theirs either. The tone, mood, and manner of the message becomes more difficult to determine. At times, without the voice sound to soften the message, the written word can be viewed as harsh and offensive. Also, because e-mail can be such a quick form of communication, messages can get sloppy. Come to think of it, I can barely recall an e-mail that I have received that didn't have a typo in it. It almost seems "accepted" to have e-mail typos. Don't fall into this trap of lowering your standards for e-mail just because many others do. Be sure to proof before you click the "send" icon. Good spelling and grammar do make a difference, regardless of the method of technology you are using to communicate your message.

Also, you can disconnect or delay the "bing"—the annoying reminder that you've just received e-mail—so that you'll have fewer interruptions and get more done.

CAR

While not necessarily "high tech," the car is a mobile office for most sales professionals. Stock it with motivational or sales how-to tapes, or soothing/energizing music to prepare you emotionally and motivationally for sales calls.

The trunk space can be organized into sections within which marketing material is neatly sorted. Drink holders, cellular phone, sunglasses, and all the appropriate accessories belong in easily retrievable places to eliminate the stress that can occur when blindly searching for them while driving. It is also nice to have a comfortable car seat if you tend to drive long distances. Another reason to maintain order and organizational flow within your car is the possibility that your prospect/client offers to walk you to your car or asks you for a ride.

Car Alarm

The reason that a car alarm is on this list is because countless sales professionals have had their cars broken into or stolen (many salespeople drive the kinds of cars that are most tempting to steal) and have lost extremely valuable (and on many occasions, completely irreplaceable) selling tools and critical information. When you leave the car, it is best to bring with you or keep hidden anything that cannot be replaced. And, of course, don't wait to hide it in the trunk until you are at the location where you will be parking. Do that ahead of time, elsewhere.

There are many car alarms on the market. Some even come as a standard or added feature when buying or leasing a car. One of my favorites releases smoke that fills up the entire car, which prevents the thief from being able to see and therefore makes it difficult to drive away.

Instant Battery Kick-Start

A must! Under $100. Lasts forever, always ready in the trunk when you leave your lights on on a rainy or foggy day. Invaluable. Mine has saved me at times when I had not a second to spare to wait for the AAA service truck. BOOSTER PAC, Century Mfg. Co., Minneapolis, Minnesota. To order: 1-800-328-2921.

BLACK-AND-WHITE PRINTER

Hewlett Packard makes a nice laser jet printer. It is fast and produces crisp, clean copies. There are all-in-one printers that are designed to print both color and black and white; or, if you have both types of printers, you can get a switch to go back and forth between them.

COLOR PRINTER

Color printers create strong first impressions. You can scan in photos or even make custom cards.

BLACK-AND-WHITE/COLOR PHOTOCOPIER

The black-and-white photocopier is used so often that today it's taken for granted. People forget that "crisp and clean" are the words that are necessary to keep in mind when using photocopies as essential sales tools. Have you ever seen a document so many times removed from the master copy that the pages just looked horrible? While making your photocopies before a sales call ask yourself, "Am I proud of the way this looks?" Remember, your image goes out with every copy you distribute.

The color photocopier is becoming a much more economically feasible tool to use. People respond to color much more positively than to black and white. Use it to bring your presentations to life. The pricing of color copies and copiers has come down significantly, and they can make an invaluable difference.

CAMERA/POLAROID CAMERA

A camera is a great little item to have handy for a whole host of reasons, the first of which is that taking pictures is usually fun! And, sending the photos to a client can strengthen rapport. Taking a Polaroid instant developing shot is even more gratifying. I once took a photo of each of my clients sitting at their desks and gave it to them. They loved it. It was a real power picture. Although many of your clients and prospects spend a large segment of their days (and lives) in their offices at their desks, few if any have a picture of themselves there.

Also, weird stuff happens all the time that is worthwhile capturing on film. I was on a sales call in the Empire State Building on the day after a high wind actually blew out some windows in the skyscraper. When the contact person kept his commitment to meet with me, I had no idea that his office was one of the ones that was affected by this freak weather occurrence. Then I walked into his 50th-floor office and saw huge chunks of glass all over his desk. He had miraculously escaped this astonishing incident, as he had been in Europe on the day of the storm. If he had been at his desk, he wouldn't have had a chance. Due to the circumstances, we were not going to have the typical meeting that I had anticipated.

He was very upset about returning to his office and finding it in ruins. The cleaning crew was on its way up, yet he hadn't had time to take pictures of the damage for insurance purposes. Then I heard my cue. "He said, I wish I had a picture of this!" I didn't have a Polaroid but I did have my regular camera in my bag. And I was off and clicking. Having the camera handy helped the prospect and strengthened our relationship. Since it was obvious that we weren't going to get very far in our meeting without a multitude of interruptions dealing with disaster recovery plans, I decided to schedule a follow-up call. At which, I brought the pictures and proceeded to navigate my way toward a sale.

POCKET ELECTRONIC TRANSLATOR, DICTIONARY, OR THESAURUS

A pocket electronic translator, dictionary, or thesaurus is great to have handy, even though your computer may possess some of their capabilities. The reason is that they work well as a cross-reference check. Not every computer contains every word variation. The pocket version acts as an additional resource. Also, it is portable! How many times have you written a thank-you note on the go and avoided using certain words for fear that you would spell them wrong? Or even worse, you relied on a perfect stranger to check your spelling! Many sales professionals report that the pocket technology is worth the investment and highly effective. The key is that you have to remember to take it with you in order for it to work for you.

BLOOMIE'S TAXI WAND

This handy invention is great to have in any major city where you would hail a cab. In New York City it is a natural. This device "hails without fail." It has a red flashing beacon of light that can be seen over a thousand feet away. To use it you simply face the oncoming traffic, hold the taxi wand up, point the red lens directly into the traffic and press the button on the back. To order call 212-767-WAND.

TIMISIS LIFECLOCK

The Timisis LifeClock is a timepiece that ticks off your remaining time on earth in hours, minutes, seconds, and even tenths of seconds. It was invented by Chip Alholz and Barry Feldner. Its creation was inspired by a quote from Ludwig van Beethoven, who on his deathbed was said to have shaken his fist at the heavens and cried, *"I need more time!"*

The time scale is based on optimistic life span averages; 75 years for men, 80 years for women. All you have to do is enter your age and sex, and the clock begins to countdown. When I told my father about this clock he quipped, "I can't use it because I'm 78 and statistically speaking, I'm already dead." Then he started wondering if the LifeClock calculated minus hours and if he would have to start giving time back now.

Instead of counting hours in their day, people who use the Timisis LifeClock use it to remind themselves how much time they probably have left in their lives. As morbid as this sounds, time is a precious resource (see more on time management in Chapter 3), and is often misused, abused, and taken for granted. The Timisis LifeClock also tells time and scrolls 164 aphorisms. 1-800-TIM-ISIS.

BOTTOM LINE — GET OVER IT!

There is nothing as constant as change, especially in technology. So stop longing for the day you will have yours all set, and embrace the concepts of the upgrade and the ceaseless evolution of innovation. Technology can also help you be better organized and more efficient, so that you can produce better results.

MAKE A LIFELONG COMMITMENT

Technology has had a major impact on the sales profession. It's greatest contribution is that it frees salespeople and allows them more time to do their primary job—which is going on sales calls, and meeting as many key decision makers as possible.

Too often, we purchase something new to help us get ahead and impatiently struggle through trial and error to make it work. A simpler solution would be to invest some time in carefully reading the directions of new equipment and/or scheduling a few training sessions to help you get acclimated, especially if you are concerned about your ability to keep up with the latest equipment. Keep in mind that your fears will start to fade away as you make the commitment.

To stay on the cutting edge, it is necessary to make a lifelong commitment to learning about the latest technology and how to use it to increase sales.

PART 3

Unusual, Unpredictable, and Unstoppable Selling

Embarrassing Moments in Sales: The Lessons Learned

Though no one can go back and make a brand-new start,
anyone can start from now and make a brand-new ending.

Anonymous

Have you ever gone on a sales call that turned out differently than you had planned? Were you embarrassed? Embarrassment is a common occurrence in the sales field, mainly because salespeople are risk-takers and many times they find themselves in uncharted waters. The uncertainty is always there.

This chapter is dedicated to sharing with you some horrifying, embarrassing, and humiliating moments sales professionals have experienced in their day-to-day pursuit of success and prosperity. Its purpose is threefold: (1) to help you realize that you are not alone when you encounter painfully awkward sales situations; (2) to find the hidden meaning and true lessons to be learned from such encounters; and (3) to laugh about mishaps (like those in Table 8.1) sooner rather than later.

Despite the fact that it is torturous to make mistakes and face the risks and uncertainty of sales, it is far worse to eat yourself up inside over them. So sit back, get comfortable, and enjoy the stories that lie ahead. After reading each story, you might say to yourself, "I am so glad that that didn't happen to me!" If, on the other hand, you can recall experiencing encounters as bad, or even worse, than you find in these pages, please contact me by fax (203-964-0580) or e-mail (jbaldridge@baldridge-seminars.com). By sharing your horrific

TABLE 8.1 HAS THIS EVER HAPPENED TO YOU?

For lack of a better word that I cannot use in this book, "Stuff" happens on sales calls that you wish didn't. But the reality is that this "stuff" usually happens to *everyone* and not solely to you. So, when it happens to you, deal with it and get over it! (Or as the actress Cher said in the movie *Moonstruck*, "Snap out of it!")

Have you ever. . . .

- Called the prospect/client by the wrong name? (and used this wrong name, not just once, but several times before discovering the error on you own, or by being corrected by someone?)

- Forgotten an important name or critical fact in a meeting?

- Spilled anything (coffee, tea, water) while on a sales call?

- Discovered spinach from lunch on your tooth after the sales call?

- Discovered a fishbone in your mouth during a business lunch and just forced yourself to swallow it out of pure lack of a better way to politely get rid of it?

If you answered "Yes" to more than one of the above awkward situations, then congratulations! You have discovered that you are human. And very much a member of the highly fallible human race. The key is to learn from your mistakes by doing whatever you can to prevent these things from happening in the future. Move on. And then keep walking with confidence in the direction of your dreams.

experiences, chances are you will feel better, and you will have provided yet another inspirational learning experience to motivate other sales professionals.

Every story in this chapter is true. (Believe me, you couldn't make this stuff up if you tried!) However, all of the names and company names have been changed to prevent further embarrassment.

I will kick off this chapter with one of my own favorite horror stories. (Yes, eventually horror stories become favorites, it just takes a while to laugh after the trauma.) I'm sharing it with you to remind you that despite all the thorough preparation you do and regardless of how much experience you have, unexpected obstacles can still occur. It goes as follows:

KEY CONCEPT BE PREPARED TO BE "OFF BALANCE"

It was the final presentation in the sales process. I was going to be speaking before the CEO, president, vice president of sales and marketing, and a few senior-level human resources people. I was meeting with them to sell them a sales training program. It was a French company in the resort hotel business. Three of the top-level executives had flown in the day before from Paris to meet me and see me in action.

The meeting was going very well, and everyone seemed to like the plan that I had custom-designed to assist in increasing corporate occupancy at the resorts. Midway through the meeting I started to facilitate a brainstorming session regarding ways to increase sales. As the participants threw out comments, I captured them on a flip chart. The group was really into the exercise and I was rapidly writing down their ideas.

After I had hunched down to write the last comment on the bottom of the page of the flip chart, I began to stand back up but was abruptly pulled back down. At first I couldn't figure out what was happening, so once again I attempted to stand, and once again I was pulled back down. I finally realized that the heel from my shoe had caught in the hem of my skirt. But by the time I discovered that it was too late, and I was starting to lose my balance.

Out of sheer desperation, I grabbed the flip chart in an attempt to regain my balance. But, unfortunately, it was attached to a flimsy aluminum stand. As soon as I reached out and grabbed it, it fell on top of me and knocked me to the floor. In shock, as I was falling down, I exclaimed, "OH NO!" And then I hit the floor. So there I was, lying in the prestigious boardroom, at the foot of the majestic conference table, with a flip chart on top of me, and my heel still caught in my hem.

The top-level French executives watched in horror, unsure at first of what was happening. Then as I was falling down, I saw them all jump up to my rescue. I heard some of them emotionally exclaim, "Mon Dieu!" "My God!" Needless to say, I was beyond embarrassed. I was completely mortified. Somehow I regained my composure and successfully finished the presentation and won the business. To this day the client and I still talk about that unbelievable moment. Amazingly enough, that awful incident actually strengthened rapport.

The Lesson

Sometimes things can happen that are beyond your wildest imagination. The best thing to do is acknowledge what occurred and move on with dignity, or use self-effacing humor if you can think of the right thing to say. (At the time I couldn't.)

K E Y
CONCEPT

SOMETIMES THE LESS SAID, THE BETTER

Craig was an industrial chemical sales professional who was always looking for ways to make contact with and to build rapport with prospective customers. He belonged to the local chamber of commerce and was planning on attending a holiday after-hours event. The holiday events always drew the biggest crowds. Craig was excited by all the top level people he knew who were planning to attend. He spoke to his wife Nancy about some of the guests he thought were going to be there. As he was telling her all the big names who were planning on attending, one name stood out—Thomas Townsend, the president of Townsend Worldwide. She said, "I think I went to school with his son Johnny." Craig said, "Really? Maybe I can mention that as an icebreaker when meeting him."

That evening Craig was mingling and collecting business cards and contact names and numbers when he saw the name tag of Mrs. Townsend pinned on her lapel. He thought this was his big chance to build rapport with the president's wife. Perhaps she would put in a good word for him to her husband. He felt that this was a good strategy. So, he walked over to Mrs. Townsend, introduced himself and said, "Hello, my name is Craig Johnston. It's nice to meet you. I'm very impressed with your husband's work. He has done so much for our industry." Mrs. Townsend politely thanked Craig for the compliment and was about to turn and speak with someone else.

Craig detected that she was about to leave, so he quickly said, "You know, my wife Nancy thinks that she went to high school with one of your boys. Do you have two boys?" "Yes," she replied. "Did they go to West Field High School?" "Yes they did," she graciously responded. "Well, my wife went to school with your son Johnny." "We have a son named Jimmy and one named Matthew," said Mrs. Townsend, "but no Johnny." "Really?" said Craig, "My wife could have sworn it was your son; maybe she got the name mixed up. Was one of them in the marching band?" "Both were," she said. Then Craig said, "Well, my wife graduated from high school in 1978; when did your sons graduate?" Mrs. Townsend looked a little per-plexed, almost as if wondering if this was some kind of cruel joke, and answered that her oldest had graduated in 1994 and her youngest in 1998. "Ow!" Craig thought. He suddenly realized that he just insinuated that she could actually be old enough to have children 20 years older than the ones she had.

Craig felt his face getting warm and he could tell it was turning a bright shade of red. There was nothing he could think to say to make things better so he said, "Obviously I must be mis-taken." Struggling for words to say to pull his foot out of his mouth, he found none. He ended the conversation with a quick cliché, "Well, it was nice speaking with you, happy holidays." And faded into the crowd. His plan to charm the president's wife had backfired. He was so embar-rassed. "How stupid! I can't believe I said that! What an idiot I was!" Craig was in no mood to continue his networking and headed home. "Wait 'til Nancy hears this one," he thought.

The Lesson

Listen carefully. It was obvious that if Mrs. Townsend said that she didn't have a son named Johnny, then she didn't! Don't try to force the conversation to go your way. Networking events have many distractions that can interfere with clear communication. Often times, the less said the better!

KEY CONCEPT — AVOID DISJOINTED JOINT SALES CALLS

Many times sales professionals go on joint sales calls with their boss or with someone from techni-cal or support services. A joint sales call can be a good thing because it can make the prospect/customer feel important and also convey a more thorough understanding of the type of people he or she will be dealing with.

The purpose of conducting a joint sales call is typically to impress the prospect/customer. Unfortunately, this does not always happen and, unfortunately, many times just the opposite occurs. I recall hearing one sales professional's account of being excited to take the president of her company with her on the sales call, only to have her bubble of enthusiasm burst when he acted bored and disinterested in the meeting, and then actually nodded off.

Another humiliating example of a disjointed sales call involved a sales rep and a technical person. When the sales professional told the prospect during the sales call that service would be up and running in a matter of weeks, the technical person appeared tense and cleared his throat as if to disagree. When the prospect asked the technician if he agreed with the timeframe the sales person had quoted, the technician said, "Well, not exactly," and then proceeded to describe all of the problems that would cause a service delay. (Have you ever experienced this type of occurrence while on a joint sales call? Did you ever regret inviting another person to your meeting?)

So, what do you do to prevent or at least minimize the possibility of disjointed joint sales calls? You:

- Create a game plan in advance.
- Share the game plan with the person from your company who is joining you.
- Decide ahead of time the role that each of you will be taking.
- Be clear from the start who will be the leader of this meeting.
- Realize that company position or title has nothing to do with who will be in charge. (In most cases the leader on the sales call should be the sales professional.)
- Create a subtle, nonverbal signal to give one another to dictate who should speak next.
- Rehearse together before going on the sales call.

- Troubleshoot in advance all of the possible obstacles and objections and who will handle each.

- After the sales call, when in the car or a nearby coffee shop, jointly evaluate what worked and what could have been improved on the call

Remember: In most cases, you probably know how to work with your prospect/customer better than anyone else in your company. Therefore, it is up to you to take charge, plan ahead how to run the sales call, and then communicate your thoughts clearly to those who will be accompanying you. It is also your job to brief your colleagues on the history of the prospect/account, and then to provide guidelines on what to say and do on the call.

Sometimes you might have to decide what is politically correct when setting guidelines, even when dealing with higher-ups. For instance, one sales professional was unnerved when her boss made joint sales calls with her because he would always be drinking a Coke between calls and then burp throughout each appointment. He was always polite and said "Excuse me," but it was a constant and embarrassing interruption. Finally, at the end of a joint call that her boss had burped his way through, she requested that he refrain from drinking Cokes prior to each call. It took a lot of guts for her to say this—but as it turned out, her manager had not realized how disruptive he was being and complied.

 HASTE MAKES WASTE

Julie's foot fell asleep while she was on a sales call. When she rushed to stand up and shake the contact's hand and say "good-bye," she started to fall over. Out of desparation she tried to grab his shoulders for support—but she missed and ended up falling into his arms. "Ugh!" she thought to herself. "Why is it that this sort of thing never happens when meeting with someone who has a sense of humor?"

Scott, an educational material sales professional, was required to write two follow-up reports after each sales call—an internal report for placing in his office file, and an external report to send to the school headmaster he had visited. Scott had just returned from a sales call at a prestigious prep school for boys and in his office file notes wrote in great detail that the kids at that school were nothing more than a bunch of lazy, spoiled brats. Of course, on the client's report he expressed how impressed he had been with the caliber of the whole student body.

Unfortunately, in his haste, Scott sent the internal report to the headmaster and put the client report in his files. A few days after he unknowingly mailed the wrong report to the school headmaster, Scott got a call from him. Scott was surprised and delighted to get such a quick response. He thought that he must have done a great job on the sales call—until he heard the headmaster say, "I think you just sent me information that was probably not meant for me to see. There will be no further need for you to keep in touch." Then the headmaster abruptly hung up. Scott felt sick when he realized what he had done.

The Lesson

Take the time to check all correspondence at least two times for errors before sending. Have you ever sealed an envelope addressed to a client, tossed it in the mail, and then regretted not doing a final proof? It's not worth it to avoid this critical step. (As Scott unfortunately realized by losing a client.)

KEY CONCEPT — CHECK YOUR SPELL CHECK

I vividly recall spelling the word "familiar" incorrectly on a document that should have read, "I am sure that since I am familiar with your organization, it would make sense to renew our contract." The real problem with this statement was that upon correcting the misspelling, the Spell Check changed the word from *familiar* to *failure*. Since I was in a hurry, and left no time for accurate proofing, I made the mistake of relying solely on Spell Check, incorrectly assuming that the word would be corrected accurately.

Unfortunately, this error slipped by undetected until a week later when I was in my client's office and noticed the letter on his desk and saw a yellow highlighted word in the middle of the page. When the client left the room to make a photocopy, I leaned forward and in disbelief saw that he had highlighted the word "failure." At first I thought that maybe I was developing a self-destructive psychological disorder. "Why would I in my right mind send a letter in which I wrote that I was a failure?" I thought. It wasn't until a few days later, when I spelled "familiar" wrong again, that I noticed that Spell Check automatically defaulted the word to "failure."

The Lesson

Never again will I ever rely totally on Spell Check without proofing. And I will allow enough time for proofing to catch embarrassing errors.

 PROOF TILL YOU DROP

Typos can be the cause of some of the most humiliating moments in a sales call.

A minor typo such as "I look forward to you reply" is not usually as harmful as a major typo such as wrong word usage ("duel" versus "dual"). This kind of typo implies to the reader that you are lacking the knowledge to know the difference. So of course the best rule of thumb when selecting words would be either, "when in doubt leave it out" or "when in doubt, have someone else check it out."

The worst typographical errors are the ones that inadvertently spell swear words or embarrassing words.

Several years ago, one of the big six accounting firms had a typo that was not caught until 20,000 annual reports were printed and mailed. The company name was followed by the tag line "pubic" instead of "public" accountants. It's amazing how that one missing letter 'l' caused such a stir.

Of course, it is always best to have no typos at all. To do this you usually just need to factor in more proofing time when composing written communication, and if possible, have a second set of eyes look at it. (Even the best proofing experts report that it is very hard to proof your own work.)

It is borderline reckless and delusional to assume that you will "get it right the first time" every time when constructing written communication. Remember each document you send represents you and your company/firm every time it goes out. And with every typo that is sent, you lose a little piece of your integrity and credibility.

Proven Proofing Tips

1. Place a color transparency over your document, or print the document on a colored sheet of paper and then proof. The color makes the document appear less familiar to you and typos jump off the page
2. Read the document backwards
3. Always have a second set of eyes look at your work.

KEY CONCEPT   COPING AFTER A REVERSAL OF FORTUNE

Joann was selling telephone systems for a major manufacturer. They were big-ticket items ranging from $200,000 to $2,000,000 in price. She called on only the highest level of business executives and once she secured an appointment was very successful in closing the deal. Joann had had a lot of experience and was very bright and highly intuitive. She focused her sales efforts on contacting the final decision maker rather than getting caught up in the trap of wasting time speaking with people who had little to do with the sale.

When I called Joann, she was running out the door. It obviously was not a good time for her to talk. Nevertheless, when I asked her the question, "Have you ever had a horrendous sales experience?" Joann eagerly replied, "Now that's something I have had. I remember it vividly."

"I was selling capital equipment. The contact person was the CEO of a travel-related company. He had led me all the way down the entire sales path, which consisted of about a year's worth of wining and dining; proposals; adjustments; much time and effort; all of which brought us to our final meeting. I drafted a concise, one-page contract that clearly listed everything he said he needed. He said he would be signing it in our meeting that day.

"I had been waiting for this moment for so long. I was trying to control my excitement. I had endured so much; endless dinners, unwelcome advances, countless document revisions, and this was going to be the moment of truth. I arrived on time and his secretary showed me into his office. After some initial small talk, he abruptly changed the subject, and out of nowhere said, "Joann, what's your sign?" Perplexed, I responded "Taurus." Then he said, "Really? I thought you were a Gemini." "Oh great," I thought, "I hope he's not going to say that he's not signing the contract because I'm the wrong astrological sign and his astrologist warned him against doing business with anyone but a Gemini this month."

Just as the CEO said the word "Gemini," his lawyer burst into the room, saw the contract on the desk, and said, "What do you think you're doing?" Stunned, Joann sat speechless as the CEO explained, "I'm signing a contract for a new phone system today." "Oh no you're not. Wait a minute here. You're not signing anything without me reading it first," said the lawyer. Needless to say, the meeting came to an abrupt ending. Joann left the office with her head spinning at the thought of what had just occurred.

At this point in Joann's story my head was spinning too. I had to interrupt her story and ask, "What *did* happen!?" She said, "Joy, don't you see. I finally figured it out. The CEO had been flirting with me and allowing me to wine and dine him because he was interested in me more than my product. In retrospect, I'm convinced that he never had any real intention of buying. Apparently, while I thought that all the time we were spending together was getting me closer and closer to a deal, I didn't realize that, in actuality, he thought that he was getting closer and closer to a date!"

"When he realized how far along in the sales process he had gotten, I think he panicked. So he devised a scheme with his lawyer to get him out of it. My take on it is that the CEO used the word "Gemini" as a code to trigger his attorney, who was probably waiting outside of the office listening to our conversation. Why else would the CEO be asking me what my sign was in the final sales call. It was a setup. I can't believe I fell for it."

The Lesson

What Joann learned from this horrible experience was that she trusted people too much to do the "right thing" even though her gut said, "there is something wrong here, I just can't put my finger on it." She's learned to ask more probing questions. "I would probably say to the contact, ' "I feel like there is something not right here, what's going on?" ' She had to remember that some people have ulterior motives and that's just the truth of life.

YOU'RE NOT INFALLIBLE

Stephanie was a meeting planner. She was going on a sales call to discuss the possibility of working a promotional event for a major magazine publisher. She was feeling very confident because she was having a good month and everything seemed to be going her way. Since she felt so upbeat and confident that day, she had neglected to prepare for the meeting in her usual fastidious manner.

When she arrived she had to wait 40 minutes to meet the contact person. This long wait, coupled with her unusual lack of preparation, threw her off. When she was finally escorted into the publisher's office, she discovered, a little late, that there were two people in the sales meeting instead of the one that she had expected. She immediately started to feel insecure and realized that she was completely underprepared for what now appeared to be a potentially demanding meeting. Her ego had gotten the best of her.

When the two contacts started shooting round after round of rapid-fire questions at her, she was ready to surrender and felt compelled to wave a white flag and give up. Instantly, the two people she was meeting with seemed to detect her lack of preparation. Despite her 10 years of successful sales experience, it seemed obvious that they viewed her as an incompetent novice.

The meeting was starting to wrap up. After Stephanie did a mediocre job of fudging her way through the series of challenging questions she was being asked, she thought at one point that she could make a comeback. However, her glimmer of hope faded upon being asked the ominous question, "So, tell us about the event you had in mind for us." Stephanie had nothing to say. She had to think quickly on her feet. The meeting turned from awkward conversation to complete embarrasment.

Stephanie was relieved when one of the two contacts graciously ended the meeting and escorted her to the door. Stephanie couldn't believe how she could let herself down as she did. She said her good-byes, walked out the door, went down in the elevator, hailed a cab and, feeling defeated, sunk into the back seat of the cab.

The Lesson

Believe it or not, Stephanie was grateful for this experience—because even though this meeting could have resulted in a lucrative and prestigious sale, she learned how easy it is to fall into the feeling that you are infallible. Despite losing the sale, she gained insight. She realized that in order to get where she wanted to be she could not let down the standards that got her to where she was, and that in fact she had to continue to raise them.

Stephanie was reminded of a few things by this uncomfortable experience. The first thing was to always ask ahead of time how many people would be attending the meeting. And regardless of how many she is told will be attending, to bring two to three extra copies of her promotional information with her at all times. Because, hey, "you just never know." (Many sales professionals, when citing uncomfortable moments in sales, recall not being prepared with enough sales materials when unexpected additional people show up.)

Most important, Stephanie realized that she had failed to rehearse the sales call in her mind as she was waiting in the reception area. Instead, during the 40-minute delay she became increasingly frustrated and on edge because every minute of waiting time was eroding her schedule for that day. In hindsight, she probably should have rescheduled the meeting after a 20- to 30-minute wait.

Always Bring Extra Copies

It is a good practice to bring extra copies of promotional materials on sales calls. There is no disadvantage to doing this, unless your promotional material is too vast to carry additional packets comfortably.

Remember That Your Time Is Valuable Too

Have you ever found yourself endlessly waiting for your prospect/customer to greet you in the reception area? When you first arrived you were probably excited, pumped up, and energized and as the time kept ticking away you found yourself annoyed, pressured by a time crunch you hadn't anticipated, and a little put off by the lack of respect shown for your time.

But, "what's a salesperson to do?" You may ask. A variety of things: You can

- Wait it out
- Reschedule
- Ask to meet with someone else in the meantime
- Build positive rapport with the receptionist
- Thoroughly rehearse your sales presentation
- Peruse the company newsletter/annual report that may be in the reception area

The point is that time is a gift and a precious resource that you give to yourself and others. Use this precious resource correctly and success will be yours.

BOTTOM LINE EXPECT TO MAKE MISTAKES— AND LAUGH AND LEARN

Remember: You will make mistakes—expect to. Eventually, in retrospect, these mistakes will make you laugh—so laugh sooner rather than later. Prevent making the same mistakes more than once. Learn from them.

MURPHY'S LAW LIVES ON

Yes, Murphy's law—which states that "everything that can go wrong, will go wrong, and at the worst possible time"—is still alive and well and rampant in the sales field. The key is not to be fearful of this fact, but rather to expect glitches to occur and deal with them as quickly and with as much dignity as you can muster up at the time. Many sales professionals naively don't anticipate adversity to occur.

The benefit (and there is one) of experiencing a wide range of horrifying, embarrassing, and humiliating sales experiences is that you are forced to learn how to approach and deal with situations differently in the future. And sometimes you don't learn until the second, third, or even fourth time the same thing happens. Have you ever found yourself saying, "Will I ever learn?!" or "I can't believe I did this again!"

The most successful sales professionals never let horrifying, embarrassing, or humiliating moments prevent them from reaching their goals. It is only when your goals become muddied or unclear that negativity has a chance to seep in. Feel the fear but don't ever let it stand in your way. The best way to deal with a tough call is to learn from it and move on to the next one.

9

Serendipitous Selling

Even if you're on the right track, you still get run over if you just sit there.

Will Rogers

Serendipitous selling is an exciting and suspense-ful way to book business, yet in many cases it is completely unpredictable. The dictionary defines the word *serendipitous* as "the gift of finding valu-able or agreeable things not sought for." So, serendipitous selling is obtaining sales as a matter of circumstance rather than a direct effort.

I first became aware of serendipitous selling while reading *The Celestine Prophecy.* This book emphasized the fact that there is almost always more to a "coincidence" than most people think. Although I never actually finished reading the book, there was one concept that stayed with me—the concept of the value and importance of looking deeper into the coincidences that occur in everyday life, and then acting on them. I can hon-estly say that I made more money from applying the concept of taking coincidences seriously than I had from reading many other sales-related "how-to" books that year.

In this chapter, I'll share with you examples of how serendipitous selling can be used as an effec-tive sales tool—but remember, its very nature makes it unpredictable, so you can't rely on it too much.

Every story in this chapter is true, although some of the names have been changed. As you read through these stories, start to think about past experiences of your own that, if pursued a little further, might have resulted in the discovery of a new serendipitous sales opportunity.

Only those who will risk going too far can possibly find out how far one can go.
T. S. Eliot

KEY CONCEPT — TRANSPORTATION ENCOUNTERS

Transportation encounters are probably the most common way serendipitous selling occurs. I suspect that more coincidences happen while riding some mode of transportation than in any other situation. This is mainly because many times, while traveling, complete strangers are thrown together. Once they find the opportunity to talk to one another, they realize that they have a lot in common. In addition to the notion of serendipity, another fortuitous concept, that of "six degrees of separation" might be considered here as well. In case you are unaware of this expression, it suggests that each individual person is at most six people away from knowing every other person in the world.

Transportation Encounter #1

One example of a transportation encounter happened to a sales executive named John while on a flight from Milwaukee, Wisconsin, to Nashville, Tennessee. John was excited to find that by putting his name on the waiting list early enough, he was able to use his frequent flyer miles to upgrade his ticket to first class. When he boarded the airplane and settled in, his plan was to relax and enjoy the flight. He really wasn't in the mood to speak to anybody.

Upon boarding, everything was going fine. The flight attendants prepared for takeoff. The pilot got on the PA system with a friendly greeting and an optimistic weather report. Seat belts were buckled, and his flight was number one in line for takeoff. Once airborne, the flight attendant started heading down the aisle with her beverage cart. This is when the serendipity began.

As the cart came down the aisle and stopped next to John and Joe (the person who was sitting next to John), suddenly the combustion of the carbonated beverages went berserk. Coca-Cola, beer, and seltzer water all started spraying everyone in First Class. Needless to say, everyone was extremely upset, except John and Joe, who both started laughing hysterically. At which point, Joe said to John, "I have an appreciation for what's happening here because I happen to be in the beverage business." "You're kidding," John said. "So am I. What do you do?" Joe replied, "I work for a company that designs packaging for beverage cans. Why? What do you do?" John replied, "My company coats the cans," and Joe said "What a coincidence!"

After an enthusiastic conversation that lasted the rest of the flight, John discovered that he could actually do business with Joe's company. The two exchanged business cards. Joe gave John a lead for some business and said, "Use my name when you call, and let me know how it goes."

Fast-forward to three months later: A new client is "born"!

Transportation Encounter #2

Another example of a transportation encounter that led to increased sales and profitability occurred to Jane Holland while riding in a Holiday Inn courtesy van. She was in town on a consulting assignment, meeting with a client who was located a mile away from the Holiday Inn where she was staying.

Since she had meetings all week and needed daily round-trip transportation, she got to know the drivers of the courtesy van pretty well. Each morning a van driver named John (a retired business executive with ten grandchildren) brought her to her clients' offices; after her meetings she was picked up each evening by Bill (an ambitious graduate student). Jane was an excellent rapport-builder, and she actually liked learning about the lives of the people who transported her back and forth.

By Friday, Jane was exhausted and just wanted to get home. So, she called the hotel at lunchtime and asked to speak with Bill, the afternoon driver. She said, "Bill, I really want to get home. Could you please make sure to pick me up at 3:45 P.M. on the dot, and take me to the airport?" Bill said, "Of course, I understand. It's time to get you home."

And sure enough, at 3:45 P.M. on the dot, Jane was racing through her client's lobby and was delighted to see the Holiday Inn courtesy van outside waiting for her. Bill got out of the van, opened the door for her as he routinely did, and then proceeded to place her carry-on luggage in the back. Jane had to sit in the front seat because the van was filled to its maximum seating capacity.

As she entered the van, she took a look around and could tell by the expressions on the faces of those inside that this was an unwelcome stop. She felt the tension and hostility, but she didn't care. All that mattered to her was that she was done with her assignment, had caught her van ride and was off to the airport, and was soon going to be home. Feeling completely exhausted, she collapsed in her seat, took a deep breath, and said to herself, "I'm done! Time to shift to relaxation mode."

Then, suddenly, she heard a conversation that she found intriguing coming from the back of the van. The business executives all seemed to be from the same organization, and they were having a discussion about a meeting they had had that day. "Since Murray isn't here," one of them said, "let's talk candidly."

Jane tried to ignore their conversation but it became too difficult because she knew she could offer the perfect solution to their business issues. She said to herself, "Stop. Just ignore it. You're tired and you don't need to get involved with this." She shut her eyes and tried to go to sleep.

Finally, despite her exhaustion and resistance to getting involved, she just had to say something. She turned and suddenly realized that there were approximately nine people sitting behind her. Trying desperately to come up with a good segué in order to enter the conversation, and not knowing the status of who was who in the group, Jane made eye contact with the person diagonally to the right behind her and blurted out, "I apologize if you may feel I was eavesdropping on your conversation, but since Murray is not here, you need to know that you need me!"

The man that she was speaking to looked a little stunned and didn't say anything. Jane opened her briefcase and took out a business card and said, "Here's my card. If you feel there might be a need to discuss things further, please give me a call." Then she noticed that the man she gave the card to handed the card back to someone, who then handed the card back to someone else, who then handed the card back to a person seated in the last seat of the van. Jane thought that would be the end of it. She was pleased that, at least, despite her initial resistance, she had seized an opportunity.

She was about to turn back around when she caught a glimpse of a hand in the very back of the van rising up in the air with a business card in it. She watched in disbelief as this hand handed the card to a hand in front of it, which in turn handed the card to another hand, which then handed it to the man Jane had spoken to, who then handed the card to her.

On the card was printed, "Walter Bristol, Vice President, Sales and Marketing." "Yes!" she thought. "The vice president of sales and marketing." Miraculously, she had reached the type of contact she would have typically sought out on her own. Just then, the van pulled into the airport and the entire group scurried out to catch their flights.

Jane was left in the van with Bill. Bill said. "Wow. You're good." Jane said, "Bill, honestly, I was so tired I really was not interested in pursuing any more business today. It just kind of fell into my lap." And then she asked, "Do you know who they were?" Bill said, "Oh, yes. They were all top executives of a highly respected educational organization based in Tampa, Florida. In those rows of seats behind you, you had the senior vice president, the director of human resources, the director of operations, and the controller, among others. The guy you gave your card to, he was the president."

Jane said, "You're kidding! I actually gave my card to the president?" "You certainly did," said Bill. "And you sounded good, too. You actually calmed them down. They were very impatient to get to the airport. When they found out that I had arranged to pick you up, they nearly had a fit. I told them I had promised Ms. Holland a ride to the airport and they were wondering who this Ms. Holland was. Did you detect the hostility when you got into the van?" "Oh, yes," Jane said. "That's because they were afraid they were going to be late for their flights," said Bill. "I knew that we would make it to the airport in plenty of time, and that I could still keep my promise to you." "Thank you," said Jane as she exited the van and raced off to catch her flight.

The next day, Jane followed up by calling Walter. He was receptive to the call and mentioned how amazed he had been with the courtesy van driver's dedication to her. He also admitted that he and his colleagues were slightly annoyed by the detour to pick her up, but now were curious to learn more about what she had to offer. Jane promised to send Walter some promotional material and then followed up a week later.

Fast-forward to three months later. Jane got the business, and Walter's company got an excellent remedy for resolving a stressful business issue.

"Knowing when to seize an opportunity is the most important thing in life."
Benjamin Disraeli

CURIOUS ENCOUNTERS

A "curious encounter" occurs when a chance meeting or situation becomes "curious" and warrants further inquiry or investigation. Watch how the following curious encounters unfold into lucrative sales opportunities. While reading this section, think about how you can increase the odds of this happening to you by simply asking more questions during such encounters.

Curious Encounter #1

After attempting for hours to sell her training services through scores of cold calls that led to countless voice mail messages with few encouraging results, Susan decided to take a break from a grueling day at the office. A change of scenery would do her good, she thought. She removed her headset, took a deep breath, stood up and went out to the specialty bread store around the corner.

The atmosphere was perfect for her: beautiful baskets, assorted plants, teapots, and pastries beautifully displayed. The aroma of fresh bread filled the air. "Ah," she thought. "This is the perfect getaway. In twenty minutes I'll be completely rejuvenated and ready for round two of my cold-calling campaign."

She went to the counter and ordered an Earl Grey tea and a slice of focaccia bread. While she waited, she struck up a conversation with the woman behind the counter. She said, "Hi! My name is Susan. You must be new." The woman responded, "Yes, as a matter of fact, I am. My

name is Lisa." As they continued to talk at greater
length, Susan realized that Lisa seemed different
from others who had waited on her in the past.
Susan asked, "What's your background?" Lisa
replied, "Training and development." "You're kidding? What kind of training?" She said "Mostly
sales and customer service. I'm here because I'm
helping out a friend who owns the store while I
interview for a new position." Susan asked, "What
industry were you in?" "Health and beauty aids,"
Lisa responded. So Susan asked, "I know it's such
a big industry but, do you happen to know Wendy
Brighton?" Lisa looked stunned and said, "Of
course I do. We used to work together at Larson."
"That's amazing. I used to do training for her and
when she left the company I lost track of where
she went. Do you know where she is working
now?" "Oh yes. She's the vice president of sales
and marketing at Kinsley's." Susan couldn't
believe it. All her hours of cold calling this morning, and the path to the real business all the while
had been in this bread store.

Susan asked Lisa, "Are you going to be here for
a while?" "Actually, today is my last day," replied
Lisa. Susan asked, "Can I have your number in
case you need training where you end up?"
"Sure," she said. Susan asked to have her order
wrapped to go and hurried back to the office to
follow up on this lead.

Fast forward to three months later: Susan is
selected by Wendy Brighton to speak at the
national sales conference at Kinsley's annual
meeting, after which she was retained as a consultant for the following year.

Curious Encounter #2

Another example of a curious encounter happened
when a sales professional named Joseph Rowland
went on a sales call. Joseph and his prospect were
engaged in a positive and lengthy conversation
about how they might do business together, when
the prospect was called out of the room to tend to
an urgent matter. While Joseph was sitting in front
of the prospect's desk, he just happened to notice
a name written in large letters that looked familiar. At first, Joseph thought nothing of it, and then
he became curious. He leaned forward and recognized the name. On a notepad in front of the

phone was written the name "Peter Carlson." It seemed peculiar to him, because Peter Carlson—if indeed it was the same Peter Carlson that he was thinking of—had been a client of Joseph's for three years before leaving his company. It had been four years since he had spoken to Peter. Recently, Joseph had happened to run into other people from the company where Peter used to work, who mentioned where Peter was currently employed. Joseph had every intention of giving Peter a call, but he had become busy and time had just slipped away. Thinking that this was a curious coincidence because he had been planning to call Peter, he made a note to himself to contact Peter later that day. When the contact returned, they finished up their meeting. When Joseph got to his car, he called information for Peter's new number and gave him a call.

Peter answered and said, "Joseph, your timing is perfect! We were just discussing user application for our next system. Actually, we have three other vendors vying for the business but, come to think of it, you might be able to provide the best solution." Joseph set up an appointment with Peter and his colleagues.

Fast-forward after numerous detailed conversations: Joseph was selected to be the sole vendor for this project. One week later, Peter was downsized. Upon hearing the news of Peter's departure, Joseph was intrigued by the critical role his timing had played and the series of events that had led to this big sale.

TRACE YOUR STEPS

Take a moment to think of your current clients. Trace back the steps that led you to them. Although by definition it's impossible to predict a coincidental encounter, the phenomenon of serendipitous selling is real. Serendipitous selling is a curious thing. Some people don't reflect upon the unusual nature of the way they obtain some of their business.

There are three key factors to increasing the odds of encountering potentially lucrative coincidences. They are (1) staying visible; (2) keeping aware; and (3) acting on impulse. Applying this formula will help you to increase your probability of success.

KEEP THINGS IN PERSPECTIVE

Obviously, relying on serendipitous selling and "chance" encounters as a primary method of generating leads and procuring sales would be a big mistake. Most sales professionals report that they consider serendipitous selling as "icing on the cake." Remember that without the cake (your steady flow of activities to generate more business) the icing is just a bunch of goo on a platter. In other words, widen your awareness without counting on what is not certain.

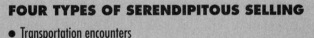

I was seldom able to see an opportunity until it had ceased to be one.

Mark Twain

FOUR TYPES OF SERENDIPITOUS SELLING

- Transportation encounters
- Curious encounters
- Opposite intentions
- Visual serendipity

OPPOSITE INTENTIONS

Opposite intentions happen when you experience a complete reversal of what you were expecting to occur. For instance, sometimes sales professionals experience serendipitous selling when *they* are the customer in the interaction.

Opposite Intention #1

One salesperson called Norco Corporation to express his dissatisfaction with his new electric shaver. His call was transferred to the customer service department. As he was voicing his complaint, the pleasant mood and manner of the customer service representative impressed him. She had not only heard him out, but also came up with a very workable solution, while simultaneously making him feel like a highly valued customer.

As he was about to hang up, he thought he should inquire about whether Norco might have a need for the services he sold. He was a representative of a training company, in the corporate training division. So, he asked if the customer service representative thought that there might be a need for customer service training at Norco. She said, "Absolutely. I would love it. Why don't you call Jim Farr in human resources? He thanked her for the lead and made Jim Farr his next phone call. Fast-forward to five months later: He sold a customer service seminar.

Opposite Intention #2

Mike received a telephone call from a man named Jerry who was soliciting subscriptions to the local newspaper. Mike had a little time on his hands, and being a salesperson himself, was curious about the sales pitch that was going to be used on him, and in the ways the telemarketer was going to handle the various objections he was thinking of giving him. So, Mike decided to have a little fun.

Mike listened carefully to the telemarketer's sales presentation. "Hi. This is Jerry. Just calling to see how you are doing tonight. I'm with the local newspaper and was wondering if you might be interested in having me sign you up as one of our subscribers." Mike then threw out the objection, "You know Jerry, in the past when I subscribed, the newspapers just piled up. I really have no need to get caught up in that mess again." Then Mike waited to hear the comeback. Jerry inquired, "So, you don't read the paper every day?" And Mike answered "No."

Then Jerry said, "Many of our subscribers don't read the paper every day either, but they love to get the Sunday paper. It has lots of interesting feature articles and a calendar that lists business and community events. It can catch you up on everything important that is going on. Would that interest you?" Mike said, "Well, not really but, you seem to be really good at handling objections. I happen to be in sales myself, so I just thought I would share that compliment with you." Upon which Jerry replied, "Well actually, I'm not a standard telemarker. I happen to be the manager of the telemarketing team and my name isn't Jerry, it's Bruce. I'm only using the name Jerry because there are two Bruces here. "Well, it's nice to meet you Bruce. It might interest you to know that I sell software to call centers. My software is proven to increase the call productivity of telemarketers. Would you be interested in learning more about it?" "Yes, I would," Bruce said, and gave Mike his direct phone number.

Fast-forward to two weeks later: Mike met with Bruce to discuss various software options. The outcome of this sales scenario is still pending, but looking good.

VISUAL SERENDIPITY

Visual serendipity occurs when there is something visibly noticeable that compels strangers to come up and speak with you. Fashion consultant Loretta Soloway says this happens to her all the time.

Loretta Soloway is a sales representative at The Carlisle Collection, an exclusive women's clothing showroom on Park Avenue in New York City. She recalls many visual serendipitous sales experiences, primarily because she wears what she sells. Whenever she is walking through the streets of New York, heads turn and many feel compelled to compliment her and ask, "Where did you get your beautiful clothes and accessories?" Loretta shared the following two stories with me:

Visual Serendipitious Encounter #1

One day Loretta was leaving work and feeling exhausted. As she walked to the front of the Waldorf Astoria to hail a cab, a woman walking by noticed her. Before Loretta had a chance to get into the cab, the woman, who seemed to come out of nowhere, said, "Excuse me. I just love your outfit. If you don't mind, I feel compelled to ask you where you got it." Loretta, who was wearing an eye-catching pistachio green jacket with a shawl, said that she was in the fashion business and gave the woman her card. As it turned out, the woman was from Vermont and only in town for a few days.

Fast-forward to the next day: Loretta had a sale.

Visual Serendipitious Encounter #2

Loretta's second visual serendipitous encounter happened during a late lunch break, while she was shopping at Bergdorf Goodman's department store on Fifth Avenue. She was going to make a telephone call. As she walked into the room where the phones were, she noticed a woman sitting on the couch. Loretta felt dead tired and she said to herself, "Maybe I'll just sit a moment next to that woman." She sat down, and had just closed her eyes to relax and enjoy a moment of solitude from her hectic day, when the woman seated next to her said, "Excuse me, you obviously have incredible taste. Your jewelry and clothing go together so well. You look terrific!" Loretta opened her eyes, turned to the woman, and said. "Oh, thank you. I'm in 'the business'." "Really, what do you do?" the woman asked. "I work for The Carlisle Collection as a fashion consultant." Then, the woman said, "You know, my husband is a plastic surgeon and I was sitting here thinking maybe I should get a face-lift, because I felt like I needed a pick-me-up. However, maybe I only need a wardrobe lift instead."

Fast-forward to five minutes later: Loretta is escorting her new customer up to the showroom.

Perk Up and Go for It!

As Loretta found in both examples, most people experience a serendipitous encounter not only when they least expect one, but usually when they are tired, not looking for it, and not even wanting it. The key is to recognize that the opportunity for making a sale is in the air, and to force yourself to perk up and go for it!

Visual Serendipitious Encounter #3

An example of visual serendipity in a different industry is provided by Ben. Ben, the founder of Immedia (as in "immediate" media), a high-tech multimedia light, sound, and video design firm, says that he got one of his firm's largest consulting assignments from visual serendipity.

His prospective client was flipping through a magazine and saw some information about Ben's firm in an article. The prospect phoned Ben and started the conversation by inquiring about the purchase of a VCR. Initially, most people in Ben's industry would have been put off by a call for such a small-ticket item and probably would have immediately referred this caller to a consumer electronics store. But Ben was curious and asked a few questions like "Why are you buying the VCR?" "To play music videos," the man replied. "Why are you playing music videos?" Ben asked. "Because I am building a nightclub," the man said. "Do you need anything else?" Ben inquired. "Well, projectors on the wall, a good sound system, lighting and so forth." (Bingo!)

Fast-forward to six months later: Ben had a $400,000 deal that might well have gone to the consumer electronics store manager.

INCREASING THE ODDS OF SERENDIPITOUS SELLING

- Stay visible
- Keep aware
- Act on impulse (Go for it!)
- Have hope
- Believe in the phenomenon
- Keep it in perspective

BOTTOM LINE **PURSUE ALL POSSIBILITIES**

Let no coincidence go unexplored. Pursue all the possibilities.

PREPARE TO ACT ON UNUSUAL CIRCUMSTANCES

Be alert to detect and be keenly aware of coincidences as they occur. In doing so, you will very likely find instances that will seem to lead you to unexpected business that you never would have attained if you had not acted on the circumstances. Neither chance, nor serendipity, or even "six degrees of separation" should be overlooked when seeking to fulfill your sales mission.

10

Relax and Reenergize

Sometimes the most urgent and vital thing you can possibly do is take a complete rest.
Ashleigh Brilliant

It takes a lot of energy to sell effectively. Many sales professionals are high-energy people. And when most of their energy finally runs out, they count on their adrenaline to keep them going through the remaining sales calls of the day. But it's so easy to keep pushing yourself and eventually crash and burn. There is always something more that needs to be done to beat the competition or further the sale. And usually it's your relaxation and sleeping time that suffers. So more than ever, it's important to make rest and relaxation part of your daily routine.

The amount of sleep required by the average person is about five minutes more.
Wilson Misner

By taking a rest break you allow yourself to rejuvenate your spirit. A rest-break also gives you time away from the action and allows you to return to your work with a clear mind and a renewed sense of purpose. This chapter will give you very specific, quick, and easy energy renewal techniques that you can immediately use to give yourself a lift.

KEY CONCEPT — CONSTANT PRESSURE HINDERS SUCCESS

Constantly draining your energy level down to "empty" can do horrible things to your mind, body and spirit. Many sales professionals are under the impression that they work better under pressure. But few have tried to eliminate irritating stressors in their lives and evaluate how the results might differ from the results they get from pushing themselves through the daily grind. Those who do decide to change their behaviors are grateful they did, and they would never go back to the way they formerly were. Those who don't, end up getting run down, sick, and at times are even hospitalized for exhaustion or illnesses they ignored the symptoms of earlier.

Here are some key concepts and tips that will help you to discover how taking time out to relax actually gives you more energy in your day, allowing you to get even more done. As is the case before using any physical exercise, consult with your physician before applying any of the suggestions that follow. Many harried salespeople say they can't afford to take the time for a break or to better care for themselves, and if they do make the attempt they feel they just can't relax. Ironically, you can't afford not to. Here's how.

PAY YOUR RENT DAILY

This is an acronym that I once heard and liked. It goes like this: You have to pay your RENT every day. RENT stands for Rest, Exercise, Nutrition, and Thoughts. If you neglect any one of these four critical factors in your life, your energy level will fall, along with your ability to succeed.

It is best not to overdo these four categories by, say, exercising two to three hours every single day, or drinking carrot juice five times a day, and so on, because you'll find it hard to maintain. The trick is to work in small changes gradually so you can incorporate them easily into your life. Nurture these four critical areas. You can do this by catching yourself when thinking a negative thought and changing that thought, or deciding to take the stairs instead of the elevator up to the sales call. Remind yourself to take a rest break every 3 to 4 hours. Grab a banana instead of a donut when on the fly. These simple action steps, done on a cumulative basis, can make all the difference in accentuating your physical and psychological well-being.

The only reason I would take up jogging is so I could hear heavy breathing again.

Erma Bombeck

MANAGING YOUR ENERGY

Nina Merer, president of The Energy Bank, based in New York City, created the system of Energy Management. According to Ms. Merer, "Energy Management enables you to focus your mind on maximizing your physical and mental energy and wellness so that you can handle whatever arises. Active and successful sales professionals with high levels of personal and professional responsibility require high levels of energy. Learn how to manage your energy, and you will maximize your productivity. By using the following powerful and portable breathing and acupressure tools, you will be able to enhance your energy level, mood, and mindset on a consistent basis. This will result in enhanced performance, fueled by increased focus, creativity, and confidence. That translates into increased sales and profits."

BREATHING

Nina Merer says:

Breathing is our most easily accessible and automatic relaxation tool.

Yet, because this function is so automatic, we often take it for granted and underutilize it. Focused and structured breathing is one of the best ways to revitalize yourself. And it takes hardly any time to do. If you take the time out to control your breathing on a daily basis, you will notice an increase in energy. Do a breathing tune-up, as follows:

Close your eyes—this allows for greater concentration. Breathe in and out—through your nose if possible, otherwise through your mouth. Become aware of your natural breathing flow. Inhaling and exhaling, inhaling and exhaling, in and out, in and out. Breathe slowly, deeply, and evenly.

Now, exhale and then inhale to a count of four (or, about four seconds); then hold your breath for four; exhale for eight; and hold for four more seconds. Just remember the count:

4—4—8—4. Remember, it's the counting that keeps your focus. Repeat this routine four times. Then return to your regular breathing. It will be beneficial for you to incorporate this breathing exercise into your daily routine, even if you just do it for a few minutes daily in between other activities. After doing a few short sets you will notice positive results through a renewed sense of energy.

Acupressure

Nina Merer continues:

Applying acupressure is another way to relax. Acupressure was originally a Chinese practice of holding or massaging acupressure points to relieve tension, stimulate vitality, and treat pain. Here are three acupressure energizing tune ups:

Exercise #1: The Hand Sit

This exercise was designed to maximize physical energy. Sit in a comfortable padded chair. Slip both hands, (palms up) under your thighs, just in front of your "sit" bones. You may be more comfortable with your thumbs out. Leave your hands there for several minutes. You can do this either in conjunction with your breathing exercises or alone. This exercise recharges you—to give you that second wind to follow through with clients; to go the extra mile. It is also great for alleviating jet lag, or to soothe tired legs or feet. You may notice that in addition to experiencing a physical lift you will receive a psychological boost. It is simple and it works!

Exercise #2: The Steeple

This acupressure tune-up is for enhancing mental energy and is best done in private (unless you enjoy exciting the curiosity of others around you). To do this exercise, you clasp your hands while interlocking your fingers, much like you did when playing the childhood game called "the church and the steeple, the pew and the people." Now, with your fingertips pointing inward toward your palms, place your hands atop your head, parallel to an imaginary middle part in your hair. This tune-up integrates your logical left brain with your creative right brain. It is a marriage made in heaven for salespeople. Use it morning, noon, and night—in lieu of coffee—for clarity, focus, and concentration. It recirculates overloaded, stagnant mental energy—"emptying the cup" so that you can fill it again.

Exercise #3: The Ear Iron

The third acupressure tune-up will also boost your energy, focus, and concentration, as well as alleviating neck and shoulder tension. If you are wearing earrings, remove them, because you are going to iron your ears. Yes, iron your ears!

Move your head from side to side. Notice if tension limits your range of motion. Do you have a stiff neck? It may be from cradling the phone between your ear and shoulder. Ironing your ears can help.

To iron your ears do this: Place your index fingers behind your earlobes, and your thumbs in front of them. Now—with your index fingers stationary—press your thumbs down and back so that you are kneading or ironing the lobes. Then, slowly work your way up along the rims of your ears. Keep kneading up along your ear rims until you reach the top or highpoint of your ear (in *Star Trek* it would be the Mr. Spock point) and then work your way back down to the lobes again. Repeat several times. Feel your ears tingle and experience soaring energy.

What you are doing with the ear iron is giving yourself a remote-control massage. In acupressure, your ear is an upside-down baby version of you. Think of the lobe of your ear as your head, the rims as your spine, and the high point as your feet. This exercise sharpens your senses, so that you can really listen; see; perceive; and feel more keenly.

Once you have finished ironing your ears, you will probably experience less tension in your neck and shoulders. You will most likely have very warm ears. You will probably also feel able, alert, energetic, and very much in the present and up for anything.

 **VISUALIZE**

To visualize means to make visible through a mental image. The beauty of the mind is that it can imagine just about anything. It also has the astounding ability to rapidly change a thought or visual image in less than a hundredth of a second. It is important to use the vast capabilities of your mind to work for you, not against you.

When taking a break from your hectic day, allow your imagination to carry you away. Simply decide where you want to go that day, close your eyes, picture it, and "presto!" you are there. I always prefer to wind up on a beach that I enjoyed during a vacation I spent on Maui. As I visualize, I vividly recall sitting on the beach, with my eyes closed and my face soaking up the sun's golden rays, while the warm breeze wisps by. In order to call up this specific visualization I call it "Maui Breeze." I know this is starting to sound like a York Peppermint Pattie commercial, but this stuff really works!

As an alternative to this type of visualization, you can give yourself what is called a "visual vacation" by flipping through a beautiful picture book of scenes that you find soothing, invigorating, or inspiring.

KEY CONCEPT KNOW YOURSELF AND WORK FROM THERE

Are you a compulsive workaholic? Or can you really find the time to take a break and rejuvenate on a consistent basis without having an anxiety attack? Let's discover your "true self." Here you will find a list of charateristics of workaholics created by Jeanne Hanson and Patricia Marx from their book entitled, *You Know You're a Workaholic When. . . .* Read them and see how many you can seriously relate to?

You know you're a workaholic when:

- ☑ You love Christmas because no one bothers you at the office.
- ☑ You wonder how people can talk so slowly.

☑ You use Scotch™ tape to fix your hems and jumbo paper clips to keep your hair out of your eyes.

☑ You consider the upside potential and the downside risk before going to a party.

☑ You tell your spouse that instead of going to the Caribbean this year, you'll simply turn up the heat in the office.

☑ You move to Australia to gain an extra day.

☑ On the beach you hide your business report between the covers of *Travel* and *Leisure* magazine so your date thinks you're relaxing.

☑ You can't understand why anyone would complain about insomnia.

☑ Someone gives you a book on chair aerobics.

☑ You can't believe it's time for your kid to have another birthday.

Although these characteristics are written tongue-in-cheek, remember that Shakespeare once said, *"There is many a truth said in jest."* If you can relate to any of these statements you may want to work toward a different way of being.

BOTTOM LINE **TAKE TIME OUT FOR YOU**

You can't afford *not* to take the time out to relax.

JUST DO IT

I realize you're busy. Everyone is busy, but that is a lame excuse for not taking three to five minutes out of your day, every day, to devote to increasing your energy level by applying the rejuvenating breathing and acupressure exercises detailed in this chapter. Try them, and you'll see a difference in your energy level as well as your sales ability.

A FEW FINAL WORDS

Now that you have completed this book, it is up to you to decide which habits you want to change in order to . . . "achieve greater sales, business, and personal success." Benjamin Franklin once acknowledged that it is extremely difficult to change a habit. But, he said that it wasn't impossible, and he invented a formula to help himself and others do so. (Did that guy ever stop inventing things?)

Franklin said, *"To change a habit, begin immediately and allow no single exception to occur."* Take these final words to heart to make the necessary changes in your workstyle and lifestyle, by using the golden nuggets in this book to continue to assist you in advancing in the direction of your dreams.

Instead of seeking new landscapes, develop new eyes.

anonymous